# Mr. MiG

# Mr. MiG

and

The *Real* Story of the First MiGs in America

by
Paul T. Entrekin

# Also by Paul Entrekin

*Mighty Hands-*
*Victory Over Adversity Through the Grace of God*
*Jasper and the Christmas Faeries*

Copyright © 2012, 2022 by Paul T. Entrekin.

Library of Congress Control Number: 2012911375
ISBN:    Hardcover     978-1-63337-679-3
         Softcover     978-1-63337-678-6
         Ebook         978-1-63337-680-9

All rights reserved. No part of this book may be reproduced or transmitted in any form or by any means, electronic or mechanical, including photocopying, recording, or by any information storage and retrieval system, without permission in writing from the copyright owner.

Cover photos courtesy of Katsuhiko Tokunaga.

This book was printed in the United States of America.

# Contents

Foreword ..................................................................... 9

Introduction .............................................................. 11

Chapter 1    The Rookie ............................................ 21

Chapter 2    Flight Test ............................................. 29

Chapter 3    History .................................................. 43

Chapter 4    Becoming The Bandit ......................... 57

Chapter 5    Classic Jets ............................................ 67

Chapter 6    The *Russian* ........................................ 83

Chapter 7    Karma ................................................ 101

Chapter 8    World Records .................................. 111

Chapter 9    The Airshow Politicos ...................... 115

Chapter 10  Swan Song ......................................... 131

Acknowledgments ................................................. 139

Professional *Curriculum Vitae* ............................. 141

MiG Firsts ............................................................. 145

References ............................................................. 149

Dedicated to
Floyd McGowin

and other aviator friends who have *gone west**

| | | |
|---|---|---|
| Billy Baxter | Joe Hartung | Bob Herendeen |
| Rick Brickert | Charlie Hillard | Dave Hoover |
| T. J. Brown | Tom Jones | Jim Franklin |
| Jim Gregory | Ray Mabrey | Frank Sanders |
| Bob Sears | Mike VanWagenen | Bob Scott |
| Alex Zuyev | Mike Gershon | Bob Maguire |
| Gene McCarthy | Bob Falkins | Leo Loudenslager |
| Slick Goodlin | Chuck Lischer | Bill Williams |
| Chris Smisson | Jimmy Rossi | Bill Reesman |
| Howard Pardue | Joel "Cat" Catron | Oscar Boesch |
| Bobby Younkin | John Childress | Gunther Rall |
| Montaine Mallet | Daniel Heligoin | Dan Sivley |
| | Stan Graham | |

*"To fly west, my friend, is a flight we all must take for a final check."

# Foreword

The first MiG-15s burst onto the scene in the frantic days of the Korean War as a rude surprise to the West who felt that Russia could not be capable of producing such a competent fighter.

Paul Entrekin similarly burst onto the scene with his MiG as the first to fly in the very competitive airshow arena after overcoming a myriad of challenges in preparing the aircraft and accomplishing the difficult licensing process, and gaining the respect and admiration of the airshow world.

The story is a fascinating tour along "memory lane" and conveys the sights, the experiences, even the unmistakable smells of this classic Russian fighter. The names of iconic aviators such as Paul Poberezny, Bob Hoover, Chuck Yeager and Viktor Belenko adorn the pages along the way as "Mr. MiG" reveals the ups and downs, the triumphs, and sadly as well, the tragedies and bitter losses of friends and fellow aviators we all enjoyed the company of.

I have had the rewarding experience of watching Paul Entrekin's fast, furious and dynamic show in the MiG, and I'm sure that anyone that saw it remembers it to this day. I also had the thrill of flying alongside him in a MiG-21 and enjoying his enthusiasm for flight and for the MiG series of aircraft! Even today with the end of the Cold War, and the present day friendship with the former Soviet Union, the word "MiG" conjures up feelings of excitement, competition, intrigue and mystery.

"Bandit", aka "Mr. MiG", aka Paul Entrekin, has put this incredible story together in a way that will be very much appreciated by "Rookies" and MiG aficionados alike through the historical context and details about the MiG-15.

This book is going into the bookshelf of my favorite aviation books!

Robert "Hoot" Gibson, Captain, USN, Ret.
MiG Pilot
Chief Astronaut & Space Shuttle Commander
(STS 41-B, STS 61-C, STS 27, STS 47, STS 71)
U.S. Astronaut Hall of Fame
NAA & FAI World Record Holder

# Introduction

It is clear by my name (Scottish, not Russian) that I could not possibly be the original test pilot for the Mikoyan Gurevich MiG-15. And I most certainly do not claim to be. However, due largely to chance, in 1987 I **was** the free world's initial civilian test pilot for the MiG-15/17 series.

Early in my career as a United States Marine Corps pilot (with Top Secret clearance), I was only minimally aware of the U.S. Air Force's operation CONSTANT PEG which maintained and operated an *ultra* secret "squadron" of MiGs at Groom Lake, an airfield within the test ranges near Tonopah, Nevada.

Later, though, because of my experience with the Defense Intelligence Agency (DIA), I was exposed to some limited information.

The site, which covers an area of about sixty square miles, was also known as *The Container*, *The Box*, *The Ranch* or *Area 51* (so designated on aviation charts) and was/is home to the United States' "black" aerospace projects—those so highly classified that they did/do not officially exist.

Nearby Nellis Air Force Base also housed the Threat Training Facility (also known as "The Petting Zoo"); a small, limited access museum that contained a few static displays of Soviet and Red Chinese equipment.

The 3rd Marine Aircraft Wing, to which I was assigned, participated in *Red Flag*\* operations at Nellis which began in 1975. (\**Red Flag* is a five time per year, Air Force directed event; part war game and part readiness drill. It is the world's most complex and realistic aerial combat training exercise complete with "enemy" forces to fight.)

When the United States received its first two Syrian MiG-17s (code named HAVE DRILL and HAVE FERRY) in 1969, the 6512th Test Squadron "Red Hats" based at Edwards Air Force Base were tasked with the performance evaluations. In an ironic twist of internal intelligence bureaucracy in which agencies often declined to cooperate with one another, the data from the MiG-15 Okinawa flight tests back in 1953 was still classified. Captain Tom Collins and Major Chuck Yeager flew a series of evaluation flights, courtesy of Senior Lieutenant No Kum-Sok, later to become Ken Rowe, a North Korean Air Force pilot who defected in a MiG-15bis from Sunan (seven minutes from the 38$^{th}$ parallel) to Kimpo Air Base in South Korea.

The United States had obtained its first MiG-21 when Iraqi Air Force Captain Munir Redfa defected to Israel in 1966 with Mossad assistance. (The story was portrayed in 1988 by the HBO movie "Steal the Sky".) Israel, in cooperation with the Defense Intelligence Agency (DIA), then conveyed the MiG-21 (code named HAVE DOUGHNUT) to the United States in 1967.

Then, in 1977, the 4477$^{th}$ Test and Evaluation Flight (later, Squadron) "Red Eagles", also had to "re-invent the wheel" as they prepared to fly both the MiG-17 and MiG-21. CONSTANT PEG operated as an aggressor style training program for U.S. fighter pilots until 1988. They flew day/VFR only. The program was declassified in 2006.

By 1977, including the MiG-23 acquired from Egypt (code named HAVE PAD), the United States Air Force and Navy (with pilots originating from the test squadron in Point Mugu, California, VX-4) had access to the MiG-15, MiG-17, MiG-19, MiG-21 and MiG-23.

In the winter of 1986 while pursuing a niche in the airshow industry, I stumbled upon the first five civilian imported MiG-15s brought into the U.S. from China. I knew I was on to something since no one had ever seen a MiG fly at a North American airshow. I quickly learned that the Federal Aviation Administration did not look favorably upon having MiGs in our airspace (an argument based on perception rather than fact) and knew that certification of the aircraft would be exceedingly difficult.

After extensive deliberation and negotiations it was agreed that the first 15 hours would be flown at the Mojave airport in the California high desert near the test facility at Edwards Air Force Base, as is the case with many experimental aircraft initially flown within the United States. During that time I was tasked with compiling data that would assure the FAA that the aircraft was indeed adequate to receive an airworthiness certificate in the experimental/exhibition category (the catch-all for surplus military aircraft in this country) and that *I* was qualified to hold the **first** letter of authorization (in lieu of a *type rating* which did not exist) to fly it.

So, it fell to me to replicate many of those classified test flights previously accomplished by the Mikoyan-Gurevich bureau, Collins & Yeager, the $6512^{th}$ and the $4477^{th}$.

Obviously prudence dictated that we should at least attempt to utilize, to the extent practical, any and all manuals we had received with the aircraft from China. Without a Navy *NATOPS* manual or Air Force *Dash 1* to reference, Bruce Goessling with Unlimited Aircraft (who imported the first 5 operable jets) located a Chinese-born graduate student who agreed, for a substantial fee, to translate the manuals from Chinese to English. After the resultant translations proved to be confusing, contradictory or just outright nonsensical, Bruce admitted that he made frequent trips to a local Chinese restaurant, manual in hand, asking "What does this say?"

Four years earlier, and unbeknownst to us, the same process had been undertaken by the Air Force utilizing an Automated Translation Computer (IBM 360 Systran mainframe) with an "optical character reader" to convert Cyrillic and or Chinese. However, upon review of the finished product it was clear that there was a great deal lost in translation there, too.

Whether the reason for the problem was a progression from Russian to Chinese to English or simply errors in dialect, was unknown. We did know that, like the Air Force, the finished product left too much to interpretation so a decision was made to utilize known amalgamated data from the straight wing T-33 and the swept wing F-86 as a base line from which to start.

Prior to the initial tests it was deemed practical to replace some of the metric flight instruments with more compatible (from the western pilot's perspective) standard instruments. The workload in an antiquated single seat fighter would be substantial enough without having to engage in the mental gymnastics necessary to convert from metric indications to those understandable to ATC (altimetry meters to feet, airspeed indications in kilometers per hour to knots/Mach, etc.).

Both the transponder and communication/navigation radio packages were replaced as was the airspeed indicator and encoding altimeter.

Although this aircraft had been assembled at the Shenyang plant in China in 1954, all existing instrumentation was clearly of Soviet manufacture with Cyrillic faces, subtitled in many areas with Chinese characters. They were referred to by the Air Force as "kumquat gauges." With one exception, it didn't really matter that the gauge was calibrated in metric measurements—as long as the needle was pointing where it was supposed to (usually within a green or blue colored arc; not red or yellow). The attitude gyro, however, and its artificial horizon was, shall we say, particularly *unique*.

The face of the instrument was blue on the bottom and brown on the top. Think about that for a second and try to visualize in your mind's eye the gyro in your aircraft. It's either blue or gray on the top and probably black or brown on the bottom—sky above, earth below. Now imagine rolling your aircraft inverted and that's the picture I saw during normal flight!

Pulling back on the stick would input the gyro ball to rotate *upward* to place the fixed pipper *downward* into the blue. Conversely, pushing forward on the stick would cause the ball to rotate *downward* placing the pipper *upward* into the brown.

This is, of course, the exact opposite of the orientation of a standard western attitude indicator and, to say the least, quite confusing during actual instrument meteorological conditions (IMC). (That Air Force day/VFR only limitation during CONSTANT PEG now begins to make sense!)

At least bank angle did correspond to the direction of turn.

The idiosyncrasies of this primary attitude instrument fostered an old Marine Corps adage of *improvise, adapt* and *overcome*. To that end I simply ignored the gyro and referred to the turn needle and vertical speed indicator (VSI) and flew partial panel when IMC.

In addition, the directional gyro had a fixed but adjustable compass card with an airplane index in the center which rotated to point to the compass direction corresponding to the flight path. For example, with the compass card adjusted so that north was at twelve o'clock and the flight path was east, the airplane index would point to 090 degrees at three o'clock. That was much easier to get used to than the attitude gyro but odd none the less.

The primary rule of thumb, though, was that I could play with the shiny switches but was not to screw with any of the red or rusty ones.

That guidance was reinforced by some advice I received from Chuck Yeager prior to my first flight. He rather colorfully expressed "Don't touch the damned TO&E (Take Off & Emergency) switch 'cause it'll blow the ass end plum off the airplane!" I never did. That one was red and rusty.

Of all the peculiarities of the early MiGs, one of the most curious was the pneumatic differential braking system the Russians borrowed from the Brits. Initial taxi tests taught that maneuvering around a congested ramp was much more difficult than flight itself! Since there was no nose wheel steering, the pilot had to push a rudder pedal in the desired direction of turn and simultaneously squeeze the brake paddle located on the stick. This procedure forced pressurized nitrogen into a corresponding rubber brake bladder which uniformly squeezed a series of asbestos pucks against the wheel drum. Early on, it was not uncommon to see smoking (and occasionally burning) brakes during long taxi evolutions on very hot days. (I melted a set during initial high speed taxi tests as did a pilot far superior to me; astronaut Hoot Gibson.) It was a delicate dance to anticipate a turn and maintain enough momentum to keep the jet moving while using minimum fuel and nitrogen to taxi. Once the paddle was released the nitrogen was vented and expending all nitrogen pressure rendered the brake system inoperative. There was no backup or emergency brake.

A novice MiG driver is apparent by his tail dragger style technique and constantly banging from stop to stop on the rudder.

Post-landing braking was another story. During substantial crosswind recoveries in particular, it was imperative to neutralize the rudder pedals and apply sustained, maximum pressure on the brake paddle. Minimally effective, it was critical on short runways (5,000 feet or less) to touch down on or very near the numbers (similar to a carrier approach to an okay 3 wire) and lower the nose wheel disregarding aerodynamic braking. Failure to do so would just about guarantee an excursion into the overrun.

With the information gleaned from the translated manuals, one critical item was very clear—do not spin the aircraft. The published emergency procedure upon entering a spin was to eject. True to most other Soviet designed jet aircraft, there was a white line painted on the center instrument panel that was supposedly there to direct the pilot to the proper position of the stick should he have some fantasy about recovering from an unintentional spin. Oddly, there was no reference to rudder position (opposite) documented anywhere in the flight manuals.

During my 5th flight in the jet and as part of the flight test sequence, I was supposed to stall the aircraft at altitude while in the landing configuration. It was clearly determined that this particular airspeed was critical and mandatory to acquire.

At 20,000 feet I configured the aircraft and then slowly retarded the throttle to idle.

With a centrifugal flow, Klimov VK-1non-afterburning, engine (copied from the British Rolls Royce Nene) providing approximately 6,000 pounds of thrust, it was known that throttle movements had to be slow but deliberate. Advancement from idle to full power or back in a minimum of about 12 seconds was critical. Anything faster would most assuredly induce a compressor stall with doubtful success of a re-light.

Routinely, however, the throttle was typically set at maximum (11,500 rpm) for takeoff and seldom adjusted (until descent) to preclude inevitable compressor stalls. Typical cruise speed at altitude was approximately .84 Mach.

One interesting point to note is that the MiG-15/17 series has absolutely no AOA (angle of attack) indicator or stall warning whatsoever; no stick shaker, no rudder pedal shaker, no light or aural warning.

I learned that the Air Force took their manual translation literally and prohibited intentional spins in their MiG-17s. One of the Red Eagles was killed attempting to recover from an unintentional spin encountered during ACM (aerial combat maneuvering).

I think what surprised me more than the lack of an audible warning horn, stick shaker or rudder shaker was the minimal buffet prior to the stall. I felt approximately one half second of buffet prior to the jet's departure (from controlled flight). While it did not roll briskly, even with full stick deflection during normal aerobatic flight, I found that it would indeed snap roll into an erect spin very quickly! Having anticipated the potential for the condition in which I found myself, after one half turn I applied the most logical correction I knew which was to place the stick on the white line and apply full opposite rudder. Recovery was decisive.

I later flew progressively longer spins (up to 2 and one half turns) during which I learned that recovery grew more difficult with each progressive spin. The worst resulted in a very slow recovery (I attempted to be more systematic rather than decisive) with a loss of more than 10,000 feet. During the violent negative G experienced during the last half turn of that particular spin, I cracked my noggin into the metal canopy seam and I quickly learned that proper seat height (managed only by a seat cushion) and a tight shoulder harness and lap belt were mandatory.

Passing 10,000 feet I was seriously contemplating ejecting and very, very close to initiating the sequence which is substantially time and, at that rate of descent, altitude consuming. The jet, however, did recover. Post flight inspection revealed absolutely no damage to the airframe, gear doors or flaps; a remarkable testament to the durability designed into this little fighter.

A word on ejection from early generation MiGs . . .

First, this is a cartridge activated seat—not a rocket seat. Like any other pyrotechnic there is a shelf life. The question one would not care to bet one's life on, however, is "When does *this one* expire?" The U.S. military had the Navy labs reverse-engineer the Soviet/Chinese cartridges. We, unfortunately, did not have that luxury. The joke was that the manufacturer offered the guarantee "If it doesn't work you can return it and we will gladly provide a replacement!"

To say that the ejection process is cumbersome is a major understatement. To initiate the ejection sequence it was necessary to lift both feet from the rudder pedals (which could be held in place during negative G loading with, *never* used, adjustable leather straps) and place them on the designated foot guides below the seat while lifting the ejection handle cover which, hopefully, had the safety pin removed. Moving the cover to the full open position activated a *Rube Goldberg-like* sequential system of mechanical levers that released the canopy lock and pushed the aft-sliding canopy up about 4 to 5 inches and into the slip stream which was *supposed* to cause the canopy to detach from the aircraft. The procedure was completed by grasping the left seat handle and then releasing the stick to be able to also grasp and squeeze the trigger in the right handle.

We called it a "zero zero" seat. Not because it was gyro-stabilized and functional at zero altitude and/or zero airspeed but, rather, we figured there was "zero chance of using it" because there was "zero chance of it working!"

As word of my experience got out to those who would follow and receive letters of authorization in the MiG-15/17 series, I know of no one who has intentionally practiced an approach turn stall or spin. So, you're welcome.

While there are hours of stories to tell regarding my many years of flying the MiG-15 and 17, one other regarding flight test is of particular interest.

During the high altitude portion of tests in the MiG-15, I took the aircraft to an altitude of just over 51,000 feet. We needed to know the actual service ceiling of the jet while configured *with* both drop tanks which I had no intention of ever relinquishing. (I had already determined that landing could be accomplished with one tank full and the other empty.)

Not wishing to duplicate my efforts with the aforementioned spin, I found 51,500 feet to be the absolute ceiling with external tanks and was quite satisfied with the result. (U.S. Air Force flight tests on Okinawa determined the absolute ceiling to be 55,100 feet *without* drop tanks.)

During descent I discovered an anomaly peculiar to an aircraft with a marginally heated cockpit in an exceptionally cold environment.

As I began my gradual descent I had no need to adjust the throttle for several thousand feet. I don't recall exactly how long I remained at FL 510 but it seemed like a relatively short time since it took so long to get there. Flight controllability was marginal with a very low true airspeed so I had no desire to remain there for long and fuel was probably approaching minimal anyway.

During descent when the Mach number began to build and I received the inevitable instructions from Center to slow my speed for sequencing, I realized that there was a problem in the power quadrant. I could not budge the throttle.

My first inclination was to check for FOD. Perhaps a small pebble or other piece of debris had wedged into the gears. Nothing was visible. Wiggling, finessing and even a good, firm tug had no effect. I advised Center that I needed clearance to exceed their proscribed speed and why. They were most accommodating as I continued to troubleshoot the situation. My clearance limit was 10,000 feet, below which exceeding 250 knots is normally prohibited. As I orbited the airfield assessing the possibilities of having to secure the engine and execute a dead stick landing, I felt the throttle give slightly. With a little more coercing, the throttle began moving freely. Convinced that the throttle had indeed been the victim of a small piece of FOD that had somehow finally been crushed or worked itself loose, I considered the crisis averted and landed normally. A thorough follow-on examination of the power quadrant revealed absolutely nothing.

The second time I experienced this anomaly I found myself angry at the potential for possibly having missed whatever was fouling the gear mechanism within the power quadrant! As I assessed the situation and attempted to associate any similarities between this event and the previous one, the only thing I could determine in common was high altitude and the fact that the jet was wet just prior to takeoff due to rain. Obviously, cold temperatures and moisture combine to make ice.

In the summer, the cockpit of the MiG-15 is extremely, miserably hot due to lack of conditioned air. Vent air, too, is sealed off as the cabin climbs.

In the winter and at altitude, the cockpit is cold—very cold due to poor heating. I quickly learned that in addition to tingling fingers and toes, the cockpit environment was very conducive to freezing.

Thus, the anomaly was solved. Moisture had found its way into the power quadrant while the canopy was open and subsequently frozen at altitude, twice. The throttle remained, literally, frozen until descent into warmer temperatures thawed the ice.

As with most of the quirks of the MiGs, the solution made an excellent argument for *Occam's razor*.

# Chapter 1
# THE ROOKIE

My odyssey with the MiG began in the fall of 1986 when a friend, former Canadian Air Force and Snowbird pilot, Steve Wallace, advised me of an article he had seen in *Canadian Aviation* magazine about a guy in Ottawa who was planning to import a small number of MiG-17s.

Steve knew that I had left my Marine Corps career and was about to begin flying airshows professionally in a Pitts S-2B. He also was aware that I was searching for that X factor or niche that allows entry level performers to get their foot in the door with show sponsors.

David Chow had contacts in China that afforded him the exclusive (or so he thought) opportunity to import these jets.

Although neither of us truly believed that the aircraft would materialize, Steve encouraged me to get in touch with the guy. It would only cost a telephone call to inquire. So, I contacted Chow and asked about the validity of the article. He assured me that the information was legitimate and that he was ready to arrange shipment. His prerequisite was to place some earnest money in an escrow account that would be considered a deposit if I chose to buy one of the jets.

He explained that the MiGs would be shipped to Burlington, Vermont* rather than Canada due to Canadian import restrictions. (*Dean Martin of Warplanes Inc. imported the first MiG-17 into the United States the next year—1988.)

My biggest concern was that I would be strictly on my own regarding maintenance.

That concern prompted my recollection of a recent visit to Chino, California—the Mecca for warbirds in the United States. One of the facilities I had seen, Unlimited Aircraft, was run by Bruce Goessling.

There were P-51s, an F-86, T-33s and other vintage aircraft in their hangars undergoing maintenance or restoration so they naturally seemed like a legitimate resource.

I had kept the business card Bruce gave me when we met so I called him to see if he could offer any guidance about maintaining a MiG-17.

Bruce held his cards close to his vest and asked a few questions about my intentions for the MiG's use. I was clear about considering flying it full time for airshows.

Bruce expressed that in his opinion the MiG-15 had a more colorful history (due to its combat service in Korea and by virtue of the fact that it was among the world's first jet fighters) and would be a little simpler to maintain than the MiG-17 because of the 15's lack of an afterburner. That, of course, prompted my response that, as interesting as that was, I had no inkling as to how to locate a MiG-15.

Bruce had skillfully led me down the primrose path and used that segue to reveal that he, indeed, had five MiG-15s on the dock in Long Beach awaiting their Customs inspection.

Whether by fate, karma or good fortune, the first domino had just fallen towards my acquisition of the world's first civilian owned and operated MiG.

I explained to Bruce that I had pretty much extended myself financially when I ordered my Pitts from Christen Industries and that money would definitely be an issue even though he was asking substantially less for the MiG-15 than Chow wanted for a 17.

We discussed my business plan and considered how many venues I might have per year and their resultant profits. Satisfied that I could pay for the jet in a reasonable amount of time and, more importantly, that the notoriety of having the first operational MiG would, no doubt, generate the natural question of where I had acquired the plane (and the answer would have other interested enthusiasts beating a path to his door to purchase the remaining four), Bruce agreed that we had a mutually beneficial situation.

The potential difficulty of maintaining any Russian or Chinese surplus military aircraft offered substantial risk. We also had legitimate questions as to the availability of parts. Supposedly, the more expendable items like brake parts would be readily accessible. But we had no way of knowing for certain how reliable the MiGs would be.

I decided to delay a final agreement with Bruce until I had the opportunity to canvass potential airshow sponsors at the International Council of Air Shows (ICAS) convention in December.

Since, at that time, Pitts Specials were primarily the staple mount for an airshow performer, I had been preparing throughout the spring and summer for a major marketing effort to book my beautiful plane for the following '87 season.

I had already sought the advice and guidance of Byrd Mapoles, "The Flying Mayor" (of nearby Milton, Florida) who had extensive experience performing in his Decathlon.

Riding his coattails at the convention, as new member number 708, I was fortunate to meet numerous airshow sponsors and get the affirmation I needed to press on with the MiG. I proceeded directly from Las Vegas to Chino and told Bruce we had a deal.

During the process of clearing Customs, it somehow escaped their attention that (disregarding Bruce's instructions to the Chinese that the jets be shipped without armament) each MiG's firing mechanisms were intact; complete with one 37 millimeter and two 23 millimeter Nudelman-Suranov cannons. Bruce was coy about it when it was discovered (he did not have a firearms importation license) but someone was astute enough to tip off ATF. Not only was Bruce concerned about his personal legal liability for the shipper's mistake, he was in a quandary as to how to dispose of the weapons.

He operated Unlimited Aircraft's facility under the same umbrella as the Combat Jet and Aerospace Museum and, as such, had inroads to other museums. He astutely made arrangements for each set of guns to be earmarked for a particular museum (mine went to the Smithsonian) and, with the aid of an aircraft diagram, quickly removed and tagged them prior to the inevitable arrival of ATF agents (who, no doubt, fully anticipated that they would be confiscating five airframes).

The crates were nailed shut and were safe from ATF who had no choice but to take the contraband and forward them to the designated museums at their own expense.

Bruce dealt with all the administrative red tape (which was unbelievably extensive) involving the certification of the MiG. The inspector for the Long Beach MIDO (the FAA branch office responsible for maintenance and engineering) had been reasonable with his inspection but the inspector for the Riverside FSDO (flight standards district office) was experiencing considerable problems with FAA headquarters in Washington D.C. Apparently someone high up in the chain of command had felt compelled to issue the edict that there was "no way that any MiGs would be flying around this country." That was among the first servings of crow that would be consumed by obtuse FAA officials.

There seemed to be misguided information regarding the reliability of the jet perpetuated by rumor, hearsay and printed "facts" from supposed "experts" who had penned books about the Korean War era. The fact that the accurate kill ratio is still subject to debate is indicative of the poor substantiation of some of those references.

Somehow overlooked was the common sense approach that these jets had been flying for more than 30 years in various climates around the globe and there was no legitimate reason to expect that North American air would change a thing.

But, various FAA entities kept creating wickets for us to go through, which we did. Eventually they ran out of reasons and gave us an experimental airworthiness certificate.

The operating limitations were very restrictive with a geographic range limitation for proficiency flying. Otherwise, flight was only authorized to, from and at airshow sites and for motion pictures and air racing. Aerobatic flight was permitted.

The actual range of the aircraft, advertised as 1,200 nautical miles, was 700 (with drop tanks).

The airplane was built at the Chinese Shenyang plant in 1954 (interestingly, the same year I was born) with parts manufactured in the Soviet Union. The Chinese were later capable of complete fabrication and manufacturing of MiGs but, only a short time after the Korean War, they were still dependent upon assistance from the Russians.

According to the maintenance log of aircraft 122073, it had about 2,000 hours on the airframe and less than 200 on the engine.

One of the prolific rumors about these jets was that they had short life engines (around 300 hours) which were true only of those produced in the late 1940s and very early 1950s. (Even though radical metallurgical improvements were achieved, some later generation Russian/Soviet fighters, such as the MiG-29, were also plagued by minimal life engines.) Although even now actual lifespan is subject to speculation, due to our regular and extensive hot section inspections it was our expectation to run well over 1,000 hours before overhaul. Routinely taken soap samples (engine oil analysis for microscopic metal particles) indicated only minimal wear.

But I'm getting ahead of the chronology. First, I had to strap it on and fly it.

# CHAPTER 2
# FLIGHT TEST

Emblazoned on the fuselage, just below the canopy rail, was my name—in Russian.

Inside the cockpit which was tiny and cramped, much like an A-4, my first impression was that I was entering a prohibited space. It was Spartan and not the least technologically inviting. The Russians had somehow determined that the interior color should be a Carolina blue and it stank with an unfamiliar, redolent mix of old rubber, canvas and other odd smells uncharacteristic of any other aircraft I had ever flown. The archaic instrumentation in three front-panel segments was logically arranged and relatively simple for even a foreign pilot (like me) to understand. There were also a few switches and circuit breakers on side console panels.

The gun sight was exceptionally obtrusive. Covering nearly the entire front field of view through the extra thick glass windscreen and extending reward to within inches of the pilot's face, there was no question that it would have to be removed. The small front windscreen was framed with thick metal as were the two front oblique windows. Even so, the optical quality of all the materials was good and without significant perception of parallax.

The front and front oblique windscreen de-frosting system was marginal. During descent (especially after cold soaking at high altitude) the canopy and windscreen were prone to fogging and would not clear with the throttle at idle. Restoration of power provided a stream of warm air through the metal tube ducting for interior de-fogging but there was no means to anti-ice or de-ice if the exterior canopy or windscreen was covered. (External windscreen de-icing capability was later incorporated in the MiG-17 design.)

Side and above vision was adequate although the split canopy seam did obscure vision slightly. Rear vision was poor (but that, too, was somewhat rectified with the rear view mirror installed later in the MiG-17.)

There was no parking brake or relief tube.

The control stick was exceptionally tall, enabling leverage during high speed flight when significant pressure was necessary due to limited hydraulic aileron boost and none (including no artificial feel) to the elevators. Fore and aft travel was approximately 14 and one half inches. It had a covered trigger for the selected guns, a big spring-loaded button for momentary activation of the speed brakes* (primarily used during formation flying) and the big brake paddle that resembled a handlebar brake for a bicycle or motorcycle.

(*The two position [open/closed] toggle switch for the hydraulically actuated speed brakes was located on the left console near the throttle quadrant and was used primarily during descent and/or landing.)

The three-position (up-pressurized, down-pressurized and neutral-unpressurized) landing gear handle, located on the left front instrument panel, had a side-locking latch designed to prevent inadvertent attempts to hydraulically raise the gear on the ground. It indicated three green lights when the gear was down and locked, three red lights in transition and lights extinguished in the neutral position. If any of the bulbs failed there was a backup indicator pin (painted in a black & white barber pole design) that was barely visible above the inboard most stall fence on each wing for the main gear and one on the top of the nose cowling for the nose gear. (Many of the aircraft had a slight cutout of the stall fence to enable viewing of the main gear indicators.)

The four-position flap lever was located aft of the left side console under the throttle quadrant. The top notch was for flaps up-pressurized, second position was neutral-unpressurized, third was for flaps 20 and last for landing flaps—both hydraulically pressurized. Full flaps (normal landing configuration) had a corresponding green indicator light on the left console. The flap system, too, had a backup visual indicator pin (also painted in a black & white barber pole design) on the left wing.

There was a backup pneumatic blow down system for the gear and flaps individually—activated by twisting the corresponding valve on the right side console.

The landing gear also had individual backup mechanical unlocking devices that released the gear doors by pulling the corresponding release handle.

The aileron trim tab was controlled by a spring loaded, laterally manipulated, toggle switch just below the left forward side of the canopy rail. Even though it was the only flight control trim switch (none for pitch or yaw) it was virtually ineffective.

Rudder pedals were set 15 inches apart with 5 and one half inches of travel. (Trim could be adjusted by manually bending a trailing edge rudder tab while on the ground.) With no nose wheel steering, pneumatic differential braking was accomplished utilizing pressurized nitrogen. Centered rudder pedals provide equal braking. More pressure is applied to a respective main gear brake as that corresponding rudder pedal is pushed. (There are no toe brakes.)

Cockpit illumination was sparse. Background instrument lighting was negligible as was flood lighting, thus making night flight risky. We added a rheostat map light (used primarily on the ground) and I always carried a flashlight strapped to my shoulder harness. Night flights were avoided although sometimes required.

The landing light was housed in the center of the nose intake splitter and we added position lights and strobes to the wing tips and tail. There was no anti-collision light.

I mentioned previously my experience with spinning the MiG during flight test. Those results were factual and unequivocal.

Notwithstanding the slight possibility that on a given day with certain ambient conditions other flight test results might differ, mine were conducted over a two week period with varying ambient conditions each day.

## THE CHINO CONNECTION

In the early 1970s, Ed Maloney had a vision to preserve vintage warbirds and began the process of establishing the Planes of Fame Museum, eventually settling at Chino, California. Maloney's son Jim and his friend Steve Hinton were among the "Chino kids" who did odd jobs around the hangars and, over time, built a wealth of knowledge as both wrench turners and pilots. Others included Bill and John Muszala, Jim's brother John and paid employee Al Redick. (John Muszala was instrumental in the reassembly of Unlimited Aircraft's MiG-15s that Bruce Goessling imported from China.)

Leroy Penhall moved his company to Chino and opened Fighter Imports where Hinton divided his time between Penhall's business and the museum. Hinton earned his flight ratings and was even eventually hired (and later furloughed) by an airline but when Hinton's brief airline career ended in 1980, he and Jim Maloney created the concept of a business they called Fighter Rebuilders. Jim died in a PT-22 crash in 1982 which was a blow not only to Hinton but the entire Chino group. Hinton went on to become one of the most renowned warbird pilots (including air racing and motion pictures) in the country.

A true symbiotic relationship existed among the (mostly) friends at Chino.

Fighter Rebuilders primarily supplied support for the museum but also drew business from a select group of other customers including Bob Pond.

According to their website, today the Planes of Fame Museum in Chino has 3 MiG-15s, one of which is operable.

In his book *MIG-15* (published in 1995) Maloney, alludes to some "flight test data" that I find controversial. He makes no reference as to who flew the flight tests to acquire his data but the results do not correspond to my findings.

In his section titled <u>High Mach Number Characteristics</u>, he writes:

> "The airplane flies smoothly up to 0.88 Mach number. At 0.88 Mach number there is moderate buffeting and **a slight nose down trim change requiring approximately 2 degrees up elevator**\* to maintain level flight. At 0.91 Mach number the left wing starts dropping and becomes increasingly heavy as the speed is increased. At 0.93 Mach number there is a violent pitch up requiring full forward elevator to keep the nose down. The force to push the stick full forward at this speed at high altitude is estimated to be 100 pounds. In a shallow dive, where the airplane enters this pitch up range very slowly, it is impossible to keep the airplane in the dive. On one dive, a very steep entry was made at 45,000 feet with full power. The airplane accelerated very rapidly through the pitch up range and **attained an indicated Mach number of 0.98 at 30,000 feet**\*."

\*First, there is no pitch (elevator) trim.
\*Second, attaining this speed would not be possible considering (unless it had been deactivated) the speed brake (aka *dive* brakes) system would automatically activate at .94 Mach.

Regarding <u>Spins</u>, Maloney further states:

> "Partial spins were accomplished from an altitude of approximately 25,000 feet. All spins were made to the left with no attempt to conduct spin tests to the right (?). **An airframe and aileron buffet occur at the stall\*** and if the stick is released at this point a spin can be avoided; however, only very slight additional back movement of the stick will cause the wing to drop in the direction of the turn and spin rotation to ensue."

*As stated previously, during my flight tests in the MiG-15bis (without drop tanks) spin entries were preceded by *minimal* buffeting. Maloney does not indicate the level of buffet experienced by his test pilot.

I have no indications as to whether these flights were flown in a MiG-15bis (single seat) or a UTI (tandem seat) trainer. I also have no indications as to whether or not drop tanks were or were not attached.

These factors would create significantly differing results.

The only other issues I take with Maloney's findings are his Approach and Landing speeds.

He reports:

> "The best final approach speed is approximately 120 knots IAS with the landing gear down and 55 degrees wing flaps. The touch down is made at approximately 105 knots IAS. **The ailerons are relatively ineffective during final approach\*** and rather large aileron displacements must be made to prevent the airplane from wallowing laterally." "The *normal* landing roll distance with moderate braking is 2,500 feet. **The nose wheel shimmys excessively during the after-landing roll\*.**"

Again, not knowing the peculiarities of the particular aircraft utilized for those flight tests, I can state that 120 knots on final (gear and flaps down) was my absolute minimum airspeed. Add a few more knots for momma and the kids with a cross wind. (*If their tests indicated that aileron control was "relatively ineffective", they had unique problems requiring resolution. This was further indicative that more airspeed was required for stability.)

My jet was stable as a rock, even in cross wind conditions, as long as 120 knots or better was maintained.

However, when I later accomplished subsequent flight tests of a MiG-15 UTI, that particular aircraft showed increased airspeed requirements for stable flight on final.

These jets, whether rigged in Russia, China, Poland or elsewhere all seemed to demonstrate *individual* flight characteristics . . . an important trait for journeyman MiG pilots to know.

There was another condition, PIO (pilot induced oscillation) that may have been related to their findings if fuel located in the main tanks was allowed to slosh. (There were no baffles to prevent this.)

Touchdown speed of 105 knots is reasonable but even landing on the numbers of a 5,000 foot runway would require *maximum* braking to achieve a 2,500 foot stopping distance. *Normal* landing rollout would require nearly all of a 5,000 foot runway—more if a cross wind is involved—and even that would require maximum braking.

(*Excessive "nose wheel shimmy" would be attributable to either excessive or insufficient nose wheel pressure, dependent upon nose wheel touchdown speed, during rollout.)

Except for my initial "Walter Mittyesque" flight where I simply flew the jet around the Mojave area for 30 minutes taking in the reality that I was actually flying a Russian fighter, the 15 subsequent hours were serious, adrenaline spiked sorties dedicated to acquiring flight data that were not only imperative to the safe operation of my aircraft but also to that of those would follow the trails I was blazing in the sky.

A footnote to that flight test experience is significant in that I would never have accomplished those flights had it not been for the shenanigans of an individual who contracted with Bruce to fly the initial series of test flights.

A retired Air Force pilot, Norman Suits, showed up unannounced at Bruce's office in Chino one day and offered his services (for an undisclosed fee). Bruce was thrilled to have a test pilot with MiG experience and agreed to Suits' terms.

Suits had impeccable credentials. After the initial exploitations of the MiG-17 code named HAVE FERRY in March of 1969 (the other MiG-17, HAVE DRILL, flown since January of 1969, had been returned to Israel), Suits had flown HAVE FERRY as a pilot for the 6512$^{th}$ Test Squadron in mid-1969.

His first flight at Mojave involved taking the jet up for a surreptitious rendezvous with a camera ship (previously arranged for a photo shoot with Michael O'Leary of *Air Classics* magazine). He was supposed to remain in the pattern but departed the area out of sight for nearly 30 minutes. How much he was paid for that clandestine exclusive we never knew. We didn't know what he had done until the November, 1987 issue of the magazine was published

His next flight was another joy ride, totally disregarding the test card.

Suits felt he had us over a barrel since there were apparently no other pilots available with his supposed qualifications and even after deliberation expressing our concern for his disregard of our mission, he was ambivalent.

I fired him after the second flight and told Bruce that I would do the flight tests.

That decision proved fortuitous because I gained the kind of invaluable experience during those test flights that, no doubt, saved my life.

On 6 August, 1987, I flew the first test flight of N90601 (later N15PE) and became the first civilian owner/pilot of a MiG aircraft in the world.

A few years later, primarily because of this experience, I was extended the privilege to join the distinguished Society of Experimental Test Pilots.

# Chapter 3
# HISTORY

As the subtitle of this book indicates, it's primarily "the *real* story of the first MiGs in America". The word *real* is used because, during my exploration of facts about MiGs and, primarily, the MiG-15, I quickly learned that there was a significant amount of misinformation perpetuated as fact by either unknowing authors who relied solely on the research of others or by those with little or no factual knowledge who just passed themselves as "experts".

When I first began to acquire information about MiGs in the mid-eighties, the internet was non-existent to folks like us so I relied predominantly on books, amassing quite a library.

Today, one can simply check online resources in attempts to confirm or label as bunk some of those aforementioned perpetuated "facts". Although I do not provide a bibliography, most of my references are from books (unlike mine) with little but nomenclatural information.

As you will discover, a significant number of heretofore perceived "facts" will either be confirmed or unveiled as hyperbole or complete falsehood.

I am particularly indebted to Ken Rowe for his input regarding the Korean War era.

And, as the main title states, it's also about my own story of becoming *Mr. MiG*. Those stories, though, account for other chapters herein.

But, before we delve into the history of MiGs, a disclaimer is in order.

Some of the history contained herein is gleaned from writings that include pre-1991, first-person stories that ring with authenticity. And, as stated above regarding many of the technical aspects of these aircraft, much rhetoric that is considered factual is a compilation of recollections and reminiscences of both Soviet and allied sources that were sparingly documented and often unverifiable.

There was a constant battle during the cold war for the Soviets to counter American aerospace technology and vice versa. Some of the most significant developments achieved from those battles included the afterburner, the sweptback wing, air-to-air missiles, ejection seats and pressurized, climate-controlled cockpits. The Mikoyan-Gurevich design bureau alone has set more than 50 world records, many of which still stand.

Near the end of World War II the Soviet Union had captured several German aircraft factories and acquired substantial technical data from planes such as Willy Messerschmitt's Me262.

The Soviet's own aircraft industry was quite capable of creating jet airplanes after the war. However, due to the self-induced time constraints and political pressures of the Cold War, leaders of their design bureaus lives were sometimes at stake which necessitated use of technological data obtained from "trophy" aircraft. All individual design bureaus (or OKBs) were shrouded in secrecy by the State Security Committee known as the Komitet Gosudarstvennoy Bezopasnosti or KGB. They were knowledgeable about western projects but wholly unfamiliar with those of other OKB's so it was not uncommon to waste time and money on duplicate endeavors.

The Mikoyan-Gurevich OKB began in 1939. Their first (reciprocating engine powered) fighter prototype, the I-200, flew on 4 April, 1940; later (in December) receiving the design bureau's first production designation, the MiG-1.

Their next aircraft, the MiG-3 (fighters were all designated with odd numbers), was produced predominantly in 1941. The MiG-3 evolved as several I-series prototypes, experimenting with different airframe and engine designs.

## THE I-310 PROTOTYPES

In 1946, Artem Mikoyan and Mikhail Gurevich were tasked with developing a jet fighter capable of transonic speeds at high altitude.

Their bureau answered with the creation of the I-300 (the prototype of the MiG-9) which flew on 24 April, 1946, beginning the USSR's jet era.

After studying and improving the Me262's swept wing design, the result was their first I-310 prototype (designated S-01) which was first flown on 30 December, 1947 (some Soviet sources give conflicting dates) at Ramenskoye test airfield by V. N. Yuganov who was paid 10,000 rubles for the accomplishment.

With a tricycle landing gear like the MiG-9, it displayed the first true swept wing (35 degrees with a 2 degree anhedral from the wing roots) which subsequently required two stall fences on each wing for stability.

It was powered by the British Rolls Royce Nene-1 centrifugal flow engine (coded the RD-45) received through an initial purchase of 25 Nene-1s and Nene-2s (coded the RD-45F) through the 1946 Anglo-Soviet

Trade Agreement. The RD-45 provided 4,928 pounds of thrust and the RD-45F provided 5,005.

The second I-310 (designated S-02), utilizing the RD-45F engine, flew on 27 May, 1948. Since the S-01 prototype had failed during low speed tests, S-02 was used for spin testing and incorporated an anti-spin rocket under each wing. The test pilot for S-02 was killed during inverted spin testing.

Early RD-45s and RD-45Fs had short service lives due to use of indigenous, poor quality materials. The later RD-45FA greatly improved service life with new materials and further engine improvements in 1949 led to the development of the VK-1 and VK-1A which improved thrust by nearly 1,000 pounds to 5,953.

Previous reference to the ejection seat merits some reflection on its history as well. On 24 July, 1947, a parachutist named Kondrashov performed the first USSR ejection.

Following production of early generation MiG-15s, pilots were afraid to eject at low levels with first generation ejection seats they deemed too risky. This psychological obstacle was addressed by having military instructor parachutists perform demonstration ejections over individual unit airfields from 2 seat MiG-15 UTI (*uchebno-trenirovich istrebityel*—formation and training fighter) ejection trainers. Further confidence was attained by having "volunteer" pilots from each regiment demonstrate ejections as well.

On 17 July, 1948, S-03 was first flown by I. Ivaschenko and by the end of that year the I-310 received its designation as the MiG-15. In 1949 the first operational MiG-15s entered service with the Voenno-Vozdushnye Sily (VVS, or Soviet Air Force) and by 1950, due to its simplicity and reliability, the MiG-15bis (the *bis* suffix meant "*second* or *revised version*") had garnered the affectionate service nickname of "soldier aircraft" (*samolyot soldat*).

My airshow predecessors in the USSR flew as a four ship aerobatic demonstration team known as the Russian Knights out of Kubinka Air Force Base in the early 1950s.

It is estimated that more than 7,000 variants were produced by the Soviets and their Warsaw Pact designees in Poland (the Lim-2), China (the J-2) and Czechoslovakia (the S-103) with service also extended to various Third World countries.

According to Ken Rowe, in 1952, battle-damaged MiG-15bis' were only *repaired* at China's Shenyang aircraft complex in Manchuria. (The first MiGs actually produced and *manufactured* there were MiG-17s.) Until that time, all MiG-15bis' were assembled by Soviet factory technicians (with parts transported by rail in wooden crates) at a hangar in Gonjoring (mid way between Shenyang and the Soviet border). Ken flew a newly assembled MiG-15bis from there to a front line Korean airfield.

Some references indicate that, during 1952, the MiG-15bis was equipped with the PPK-1 G-suit system which activated from 1.75-8 Gs. Ken Rowe emphasized that during the war no Soviet, Chinese or Korean MiG-15s had them.

After the Korean War the MiG-15 was given the NATO designation of Falcon. Further review deemed that code name too formidable which prompted the subsequent designation of Fagot.

Prior to that, the first airborne encounter with a MiG occurred on November 1st, 1950, when a flight of allied P-51 Mustangs patrolling the Yalu River were fired upon by 6 Soviet piloted MiGs bearing Chinese insignia.

The first airborne victory was seven days later on November 8th when Lieutenant Russell Brown, escorting a flight of B-29s in his P-80, shot down a Chinese MiG who was diving away in confusion from his six-plane attack formation.

It is highly regarded that in 1953, (with arguably no U.S. government involvement) some U.S. citizens who were former OSS (Office of Strategic Services – the predecessor of the CIA) members raised the funding and plotted to arrange for a pilot to defect in a MiG-15.

Regardless of how it was set up, on 5 March, 1953 (ironically, the day Josef Stalin died), Polish Air Force Lieutenant Franciszek Jarecki and 3 others took off from their base in Slupsk. Jarecki broke away from the flight and diverted to the Danish island of Bornholm, a few minutes away, where he landed in a pasture.

The aircraft was partially disassembled and studied there in Denmark followed by its return via ship to Poland a few weeks later.

Frank Jarecki immigrated to the United States where he was granted U.S. citizenship and reportedly awarded $50,000 for being the first person to defect in a MiG-15. According to his company website (jareckivalves.net) he lived in Erie, Pennsylvania, until his death in 2010.

# OPERATION MOOLAH

Following the success of that campaign, the U.S. Air Force's psychological warfare section began an effort to entice pilots to defect with a MiG.

The U.S. and their allies scattered paper leaflets which offered a $100,000 reward and political asylum to anyone who would deliver a MiG-15 to our control.

Superimposed over a MiG-15 drawing and including a photo of Polish Lt. Jarecki, the text of page 1 of the leaflets was as follows:

*"This message is from the Americans to any jet pilot who can read Chinese. If you know such a person, please give it to him. It tells him how to escape to the UN Forces.*
*To: Courageous Jet Pilots*
*Subject: Flying Toward the Road of Freedom*

*The Far East Command U.S. Forces is offering the utmost aid to all pilots who desire freedom and want to lead a better, honorable life.*

*The Far East Command guarantees your safety and guarantees your living in a country without Communist domination. If you desire to keep your name in permanent secrecy, the Far East Command will comply with your wish.*

*Jet Pilots! Your bold action not only gains freedom for yourself and gives you an opportunity to live for a long time without suffering and terror from the government, but also, because of your determination and courage, helps all righteous people who are fighting against the people's enemy for the liberation of people from the enslavement of Communist dictatorship by showing them the road to freedom.*

*Any pilot who delivers a modern, complete, combat-type jet aircraft in flyable condition to the UN Forces in South Korea, the Far East Command will reward 50,000 US dollars. The first pilot who delivers such a jet aircraft to the free world will receive an additional bonus of 50,000 US dollars for his bravery.*

*Pilots, who desire to free themselves from the Communist yoke, follow the following instructions flying to land safely in South Korea:*

*Escapee pilots will fly to Paengyong-do Island, approximately fifty (50) kilometers south of Chodo Island. From Paengyong-do escapee pilot will proceed to Kimpo Air Base at 6100 meters altitude, descend over Kimpo Air Base, and proceed to make an immediate landing. UN aircraft will accompany escapee, remaining always above and to the rear. If low clouds or visibility prevent escapee from locating Kimpo Air Base and if escapee is unable to make a visual let-down, he will proceed to the Seoul area at 6100 meters and circle with his gear down.*

*A UN aircraft will then fly close abreast and lead the way to the landing field. Upon initial contact with UN aircraft, or if at any time UN aircraft attempt attack, escapee will immediately lower landing gear and rock his wings violently.*

*The free world awaits your arrival."*

Page 2 text includes General Mark W. Clark's signature and concludes:

*"Courageous Pilots!*

*If you like freedom . . .*
*If you have courage . . .*
*If you want to live a better, honorable life . . .*

*This is your opportunity of once in a thousand years! Free yourself from the Communist tyranny! Fly your jet toward the free world!*

*Courageous pilots! The Far East Command U.S. Forces is offering the divine freedom to all brave pilots who desire freedom and want to lead a better, honorable life.*

*General Mark W. Clark, Commander-in-Chief, Far East, guarantees your political, spiritual and material protection and guarantees human dignity and care. The Far East Command completely guarantees keeping in secret your name. There is a reward of 50,000 US dollars for the bravery of any pilot who delivers a modern, operational, combat-type jet aircraft in flyable condition to the UN side. The first pilot who delivers such a jet aircraft to the UN side will receive an additional reward of 50,000 US dollars.*

*On the other side of this leaflet, there is a letter pointing out to you the instructions to the road of freedom.*

*AFTER READING THE INSTRUCTIONS, FLY TO FREEDOM ACCORDINGLY.*

*FREEDOM AND REWARD WAIT FOR YOU!*

*This is the picture of a Polish Air Force lieutenant who, piloting a Soviet-made MiG-15 jet, flew and escaped from the iron curtain and landed safely undamaged on the Danish island of Bornholm. He received political asylum and is now living comfortably in England. He did it—so can you!*

And so it was that on the auspicious morning of 21 September, 1953, Senior Lieutenant No Kum-Sok, a North Korean Air Force pilot, took off alone from Sunan Air Base near Pyongyang (thirteen minutes flying time from the border—not the 38$^{th}$ parallel until after the armistice) for a routine mission. Then 21 with two years of combat experience and more than 100 missions in the MiG-15, he had been educated at the North Korean Naval Academy and joined the Air Force at 18 years old. He was with the first NKAF MiG-15 squadron to enter combat at 19 in November, 1951.

Ironically, No indicated neither he nor any other pilots were aware of the leaflets or the offers of reward and asylum. In addition, they had no concept of the value of the American dollar.

Following immigration to the United States he was integrated into society with a temporary visitor's visa and, five years later (after political intervention) was allowed to apply for U. S. citizenship. He changed his name to Kenneth Rowe and graduated from the University of Delaware with a degree in engineering. He has since been employed in the aerospace industry and is now retired from Embry Riddle Aeronautical University in Daytona Beach where he and his family reside nearby.

I like Ken and although we've spoken by phone and have corresponded thanks to our mutual friend, Floyd McGowin, we have never met. I hope we rectify that some day.

To read a detailed account of Ken's story, his memoir (published in 1996) is titled *A MiG-15 to Freedom*.

*Operation Moolah leaflet (front)*

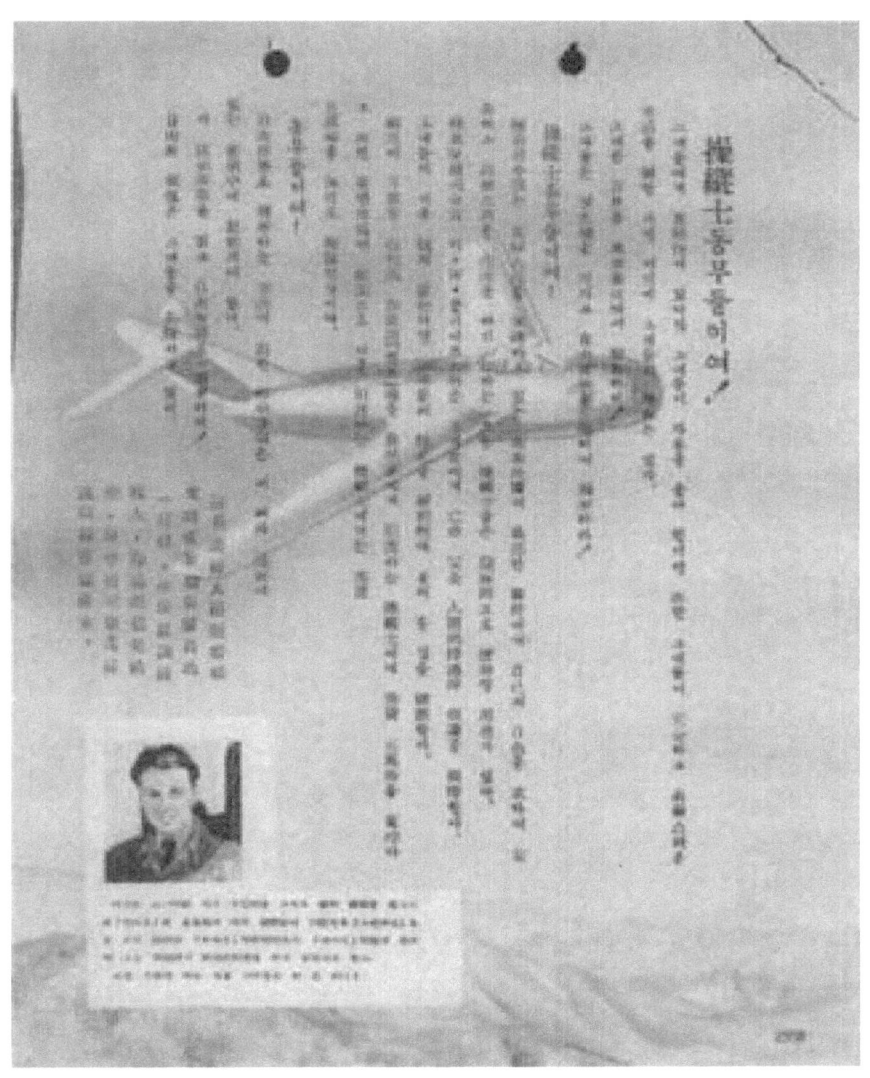

*Operation Moolah leaflet (back)*

## OKINAWA FLIGHT TESTS

Although there may be some misconceptions as to who was actually the first American to fly a MiG, Ken Rowe states in his book that on 29 September, 1953, the honor went to Captain Tom Collins.

I have read more than one account (ref. Ed Maloney, *Russian MiG-15* and Ray Wagner, March 1988 article *MiG-15* in *Aerospace Historian* magazine) indicating that the first American pilot chosen to fly that aircraft was Lieutenant Colonel Eugene M. Sommerich which is, apparently, untrue.

Following Collins was Major Chuck Yeager and the third flight was accomplished by Major General Albert Boyd. A total of eleven test flights were accomplished at Kadena Air Force Base on Okinawa. After the jet was disassembled and shipped to Wright-Patterson Air Force Base near Dayton, Ohio, more tests were accomplished until it was damaged in 1956 by a British Royal Navy pilot.

It was then refurbished and now resides there at the Air Force Museum.

It has the distinction of being the first MiG ever flown by Americans and the first MiG flown in the United States.

## CHAMPLIN & GOESSLING

I mentioned earlier in the Introduction, to the extent available, the programs operated by the Air Force, primarily in the 70s.

Of significance next was the procurement of MiGs by civilians.

Then came Doug Champlin doing business as the Champlin Fighter Museum in Mesa, Arizona.

In November of 1985 Champlin took delivery of the first three MiG-15s ever imported by a civilian entity in the free world. Those three aircraft were purchased from the Chinese government and not intended for flight. They were sold or traded to the San Diego Aerospace Museum, the National Air and Space Museum in Washington, D.C. and the Marine Corps Museum in Quantico, Virginia.

Following Champlin's lead, Bruce Goessling who was managing Unlimited Aircraft and the Combat Jet and Aerospace Museum in Chino, California, acquired investors and made a trip to Shenyang, China.

Since the United States Department of State had normalized relations with China and significantly relaxed importation restrictions on goods, Champlin and Goessling were the first two civilians to successfully attempt to *legally* import the communist's surplus military jet aircraft.

Goessling went to China and was driven to an airfield in a bus with blacked-out windows where he was told he could select any aircraft he desired. He indicated there were MiG-15s, MiG-17s, MiG-19s, MiG-21s and MiG-23s located there but he was primarily interested in the MiG-15s. He gave cursory inspections to several aircraft and then reviewed logbooks to the extent possible prior to choosing five for purchase. He eventually also purchased a MiG-19 as well.

Those original five jets were crated and shipped to the port of Long Beach, California where Goessling took delivery. When I first contacted him in the latter part of 1986 and inquired about MiG-17 maintenance, Goessling had managed to keep the shipment quiet and low key so as to avoid attention that might complicate the importation process. He was clearly surprised by my phone call which was quite coincidental.

Working quietly at the same time was Al Redick, operating since 1979 as CIA (Classics In Aviation) out of the Reno-Stead airport. Al had obtained a contract with the U.S. Air Force after convincing them that he had exclusive commercial access to MiGs from the former Eastern Bloc. In and of itself, that was true. But what the Air Force *didn't* know was that MiGs were also available from China as evidenced by the acquisitions by Champlin and Goessling. Redick's resources were in or through Poland.

Bruce even shared some data with Al after Redick received his initial aircraft manuals in Polish and had translation issues.

Even though there was some cooperation, it was clear that a rivalry definitely existed between the two. This is still evident today as a review of their company website reveals some deceptively inaccurate statements such as "Alby and his dad were the first to import Soviet MiGs into the United States." An argument could be made that Goessling's MiGs, manufactured in the Soviet Union although assembled at the Shenyang plant in China, were Soviet, too. Whether Redick's MiGs were manufactured in the USSR or in an Eastern Bloc country is semantic when it comes to the Soviet tag.

Goessling was, in fact, the first to import and make operational these types of jets.

Further, Redick's website states "Aviation Classics literally wrote the book on operation and maintenance of the MiGs for the FAA."

No doubt they translated maintenance and flight manuals which were utilized for FAA certification of their aircraft but, obviously, by virtue of the fact that *Unlimited Aircraft's* jet flew first and obtained the first operating certificate, their efforts merely duplicated ours.

Shortly after the culmination of the efforts undertaken to translate manuals into useable data, the initial flight test documents were declassified by the U.S. government after efforts by former Navy & Air National Guard pilot and astronaut Senator Jake Garn. Up until that time, there was little historic data available except in such heavily redacted form that it was rendered virtually useless.

Later, in 1989, Al's son, Alby, took over the business and I was a customer with them on more than one occasion. They had a much better parts supply than Goessling with well trained mechanics and Alby was efficient. The company name was later changed to Aviation Classics.

Much of John Penney's MiG access came through the Redick operation and John has become well known not only for his air racing but warbird expertise (particularly MiGs) as well.

CHAPTER 4

# BECOMING THE BANDIT

Unlike some of my contemporaries, I can't say that as a child I entertained the dream of becoming a pilot.

Even after graduating from college I wasn't certain what I wanted to do professionally with my life.

After operating a forklift on the graveyard shift at the Amoco Chemical Plant in Decatur, Alabama, followed by a brief stint selling insurance for Metropolitan Life, by chance I stumbled upon the name of the Marine Corps Officer Selection Officer in Birmingham during a conversation with my girl friend's college roommate's father, an officer in the Marine Corps reserve.

That conversation was the precursor to my initial interview, during which I was asked, first and foremost, why I wanted to be a Marine. That was an easy question for me to answer and I was happy to be able to express the admiration I had always held for my grandfather and the desire I had to follow in his footsteps.

My grandfather had been a Marine and served bravely in the Haitian Campaign of the 1920s where he was awarded the Navy Cross (the next highest honor for valor to the Congressional Medal of Honor).

His citation is as follows:

### Private Emery L. Entrekin, USMC

*"For extraordinary heroism in the line of his profession in Haiti, May 19, 1920. With total disregard of personal danger he attacked, with Captain Jesse L. Perkins, and two other enlisted men, a band of about seventy five armed bandits of the Mirebalis District, resulting in the death of the greatest bandit leader, Benoit Batraville, and the practical suppression of banditry throughout the District."*

That brief description doesn't do justice to the significance of Grandpa's achievement, so allow me to provide a brief history lesson.

Sometime during 1919 in Haiti, Charlemagne Massena Peralte was in control of a rebel army of Cacos. To assist the Haitian government with regaining control of the countryside, the Second Marine Regiment of the First Marine Brigade was sent there along with a detachment from Squadron E, flying 7 Curtiss HS-2s and 6 Curtiss Jennies.

Shortly after their arrival, two recon Marines and a gendarme (a Haitian government soldier) got past six Caco outposts and into Charlemagne's camp where they killed him. The Marines lashed his body across a mule and packed him down into the city of Cap Haitien. Benoit Batraville took his place.

On 14 January, 1920, Batraville infiltrated 300 men into Port-au-Prince. By the morning of the 15th, 66 were dead and twice that many wounded. Over 3,000 Cacos eventually surrendered during January and February but Batraville would not concede.

Marine pilots were experimenting with bombing by dropping them out of mail sacks tied to their landing gear spreaders. Eventually they had bomb racks and achieved good accuracy at 45 degree dive angles. In March, two Marine aircraft caught Batraville and his rebels on a hilltop near Mirebalis and drove him into the gunfire of the converging Marine ground patrol. Batraville escaped but lost 200 more men. On 4 April, 1920, Batraville ambushed a Marine patrol and later ceremonially ate the heart and liver of the lieutenant in charge.

When the word of this atrocity made its way back to the Marines, they were enraged and even more determined to locate and destroy the enemy.

A few weeks later Batraville had the misfortune of making the acquaintance of my grandfather and his patrol.

And so it was that I was destined to become a Marine—even today, to the core of my being, I am . . . Marine.

But, I still hadn't considered flying.

When I was administered the initial battery of qualifying tests to go to OCS (Officer Candidates School), I also scored well enough on the flight assessment portion to be offered an aviation guarantee; the promise that I would be sent to flight training if commissioned as a second lieutenant and, if I could pass the physical.

I did both and a few months later found myself in Pensacola preparing to fly the T-34C.

I never got a down in flight school (although I may have deserved one) and my grades were very good. I was on my way to flying the F-4 Phantom—my dream jet. That dream evaporated at selection time, though, when I was informed that due to "the needs of the Marine Corps" the jet pipeline was closed and I would be flying helicopters. The good news, they said, was that I could pick whichever I wanted so I accepted my fate and temporarily exchanged my dream of flying fast for being able to fly backward.

Upon receipt of my "Wings of Gold" I was selected to fly the UH-1N Huey at Camp Pendleton, California and, surprisingly, absolutely loved it.

After becoming qualified in the N model, I was assigned to the HML-267 Stingers. My next assignment was the Gunfighters of HMA-369 when the Marine Corps decided to composite their UH-1N and AH-1J squadrons. Eventually, all HMA (Helicopter Marine Attack) and HML (Helicopter Marine Light) squadrons were designated as HMLA (Helicopter Marine Light Attack).

Upon leaving Camp Pendleton, I received orders for flight instructor duty with my old squadron, the VT-3 Red Knights.

It was not uncommon to fly more than 100 hours a month including cross-country flights on weekends. It was during these cross-countries (typically to an airshow site as a static display) that I met and became friends with many airshow pilots.

I went to Oshkosh and Abbottsford (British Columbia), Reno and Moose Jaw (Saskatchewan) and other points from El Paso to Nova Scotia. My students loved it and so did I.

If I'd had the option, I would have gladly remained a captain in the Marine Corps and instructed in the T-34 until retirement. It was, by far, my most rewarding posting.

But, even though I was led to believe that my next duty station would be fixed wing and I had every intention of being a career Marine, that old "needs of the Marine Corps" logic, again, interceded and threw *my* plans a curveball.

Usually, Marines salute smartly, say "Aye aye, sir" and carry out their assignment. Usually.

In this case, my secondary MOS as a forward air controller had, supposedly, fostered the aviation monitor at HQMC to select me for an air officer billet with a battalion. He further expounded that I could anticipate these orders as a 3 year tour which, to my thinking, was unacceptable. Three years out of the cockpit as a junior Major followed by transition training to a fixed-wing squadron as a mid to senior Major did not seem career enhancing to me.

It was time for a gut check.

I tendered my resignation from active duty but retained a reserve commission and took a leap of faith that I could make a career of the airshow business. The biggest question was how.

Another Marine and I had considered the idea of creating a formation aerobatic team and we both agreed to a concept and a loosely formed business plan. Unfortunately, that plan never came together because of his personal issues and I was left to fend for myself as a solo act.

By the end of May, 1986, my Pitts S-2B was delivered from the factory in Afton, Wyoming. Following a beautiful paint job in Santa Paula, California, and some upgraded instrumentation by the Ray Ban Gold Team's mechanic, Fred Beauchesne in Langley, British Columbia, the "Spectrum Eagle" was ready to go.

And so was I, following some outstanding aerobatic advice and instruction from my Pitts mentor, Dan Gray. Although I had been an aerobatic instructor, I had limited tail-dragger time and the things I learned about inverted flat spins and other maneuvers the military didn't teach were lifesavers.

It was during all this work up time, preparing for the 1987 airshow season, that I made that fortuitous phone call to David Chow and shifted gears from the Pitts to the MiG.

Although my call sign in the Marine Corps had varied from squadron to squadron, it was inevitable that by virtue of flying a formerly hostile Russian jet I would eventually be labeled by my contemporaries as *Ivan*, *Boris* or some such moniker. I was more than pleased when some settled on *Bandit*, though, and it stuck. (I later learned that each of the 69 pilots in the 4477th Test and Evaluation Squadron who flew MiGs under CONSTANT PEG had a *Bandit* number. Thus, it was a privilege to be considered by the same name.)

Sadly, my jet suffered a much less dignified fate being labeled with the NATO code name of Fagot.

Immediately after all the flight tests were complete and certification hurdles had been cleared, I was ready to take the MiG on the road for our first flight demonstration in August of 1987. It was the culmination of eight months of intense political lobbying and diligent application of all the piloting skills I could muster.

Appropriately, the first display would take place at the Abbotsford International Airshow in British Columbia, Canada; at that time, the premier airshow in Canada.

Since, for some reason, I deduced that utilizing the drop tanks would not be necessary for the trip up the west coast from Chino, I had filed to stop for fuel at Paine Field in Seattle but instead was forced to land at SEA TAC where, despite a gentle touchdown, my nose tire blew (due to a loose rim) on rollout.

With some expedited shipping via FedEx and the cooperation of a local A&P, I was on my way in a matter of hours and flew my first airshow in the MiG.

Although I had what I thought was a very good flight sequence planned and rehearsed, the folks at Abbotsford requested that I fly with Ben Hall.

Ben owned the only flying F-86A in existence so it was appropriate for us to take advantage of the opportunity to fly a historically significant display.

Ben was a good pilot and already had an idea for a mock dogfight which proved to be outstanding.

We flew together again the following weekend for a show sponsored by the Lynnwood Rotary Club at Paine Field in Everett, Washington. That was the MiG's debut airshow in the United States.

There was a significant difference in that airshow performance, though.

In order to fly aerobatics at an airshow, the pilot is required to meet some qualifications including possessing a current aerobatic competency card. This critical designation is received following a satisfactory demonstration of these abilities for (at that time) an FAA inspector. The *Catch 22* in this requirement is that the evaluated demonstration must be flown at the altitude requested by the applicant in waivered airspace but the demonstration cannot be flown in waivered airspace without the card.

Fortunately for me, Mr. Bob Norton both understood and appreciated my dilemma and cleared me to fly tail chase in a three ship flight demonstration with Ben and Terry Kriha, a Boeing test pilot flying an F-86 camera ship. We completed the airshow with a couple of loose formation fly-bys and I was greeted on the ground by Bob smiling and handing me my first aerobatic competency card.

That would be impossible under today's tightly regulated procedures.

With the notoriety of flying the only operable MiG-15 in the free world, I was booked for an airshow every weekend for the remainder of the season.

Surplus military jet aircraft, although not unusual, were not commonplace around the 'airshow circuit" at that time. There were local T-33s, the odd F-86 and a few other "jet warbirds" that flew locally or regionally but the conventional wisdom at the time was that it was a money losing venture to try to fly nationally. I was told by *experts* more than once "You can't do that." Following my first successful and profitable season I was asked by those same *experts* "How'd you do that?"

A smarter businessman would have maintained all the flight test data as well as his business plan as proprietary, but I was young, proud and foolish and ignorantly spilled my guts about every detail. Although my intentions were altruistic, sharing that information enabled my inevitable competition, albeit minimal, to expedite their plans which would prove to be ruthless. It wasn't personal; just business.

Even so, from an entertainment perspective my learning curve was still steep. I already knew the importance of engaging the audience with both a visual and audible attention sustaining performance. The MiG's smoke system was second to none pumping out 50 gallons of smoke oil during a 12 minute routine. The aerobatics were low level with horizontal maneuvers executed at altitudes varying from ground level to 500 feet. The only vertical maneuvers I included were a ½ Cuban and a loop.

I brought my own taped narration and music, artfully crafted by a local Pensacola radio personality, Dan Lucas.

I also carried a tape with only music that was used on the occasions I had the luxury of working with a professional announcer like Frank Kingston Smith, Danny Clisham and even the magnificent Johnny Kazian. The majority of airshows, though, did not employ such high caliber professionals and instead relied on local aviation aficionados or personalities.

I crossed the North American continent multiple times and flew from the extremes of Gander, Newfoundland to San Diego and from Abbottsford, British Columbia to Puerto Rico.

# Chapter 5
# CLASSIC JETS

Just prior to the start of our flight test phase, I learned from Bruce that one of the other four MiG-15s had been purchased by Jim Robinson.

Jim already had an awesome collection of jet warbirds at his facility in Houston and understood the complexity of our endeavor to get the jets certificated. Jim was extremely likable and humble. With a quick smile and enthusiasm for aviation he was also very smart when it came to operating jet aircraft safely. He surrounded himself with some of the best mechanics and pilots in the country to fly the Combat Jet Museum's aircraft, meticulously hangared and maintained at Hobby airport.

Jim's chief pilot was Ed Schneider. Ed had served as a Navy pilot and was employed by NASA as a test pilot at Edwards Air Force Base. He had an extensive background in both helicopter and fixed wing aviation.

Also flying as project pilots were Hoot Gibson and Chuck Scott, also former naval aviators.

Hoot was an astronaut and Chuck flew for Southwest Airlines.

Over time, I also became a project pilot for the Combat Jet Museum, occasionally flying Jim's MiG-15 while Ed was the primary pilot for the Hawker Hunter. Hoot flew the MiG-21 (the first one flown in America and obtained through Dean Martin of Warplanes, Inc. in 1990) and Chuck flew either of the two F-86s and the A-4.

Of course Jim was checked out in all his jets which also included an F-104 Starfighter and a T-33.

My favorite story involving flying with Chuck and Eddie took place during a trip from Hobby to Addison, Texas and back.

Weather was marginal around Houston at low altitudes but was forecast as VFR on top. Chuck was the flight lead in an F-86 and Ed flew the bright red Hunter on Chuck's left wing. I flew the MiG-15 on the right.

I believe this was my first flight in this MiG and was unfamiliar with a minor glitch in its canopy system. My MiG required only a gentle push forward to close and lock the canopy. This one needed an additional tug to ensure the canopy was in the proper position to seal when pressurized and the very small gap was not visible from a normal seating position.

During climb out, we were all concentrating intently as we flew in close formation to maintain visual contact. Chuck did an outstanding job during the brief and as flight lead made all the radio calls and allowed adequate time for frequency changes and check-ins. His power changes were subtle and his lead platform was rock solid.

Just prior to level-off I began to experience symptoms of hypoxia.

I told the guys my situation and after a quick assessment of the problem I switched to 100% oxygen and we proceeded uneventfully.

While in Addison we participated in an air to air photo session for a highly acclaimed warbird magazine which resulted in some beautiful photographs.

The formation flying with Chuck and Eddie was tremendously fun due in no small part to the fact that I flew with a couple of consummate professionals. Our training as naval aviators was still fresh and we became fast friends.

We also flew together at Oshkosh.

A notable story from one of those flights involved Hoot and me. With me leading in a MiG-15, Hoot joined on me in a MiG-21; a never before seen photo opportunity at arguably the premier civilian airshow event in the world.

On one particular pass we were arching by the crowd line at 300 feet and 300 knots. Hoot was in immaculate position on my right wing and really tight. We were later accused of touching during that pass (which, of course, we did not) because of the optical illusion of a sequence of rapidly shot photos. It was truly a thing of beauty.

Like me, Hoot, Chuck and Ed are all now retired but their legacy as unparalleled pilots is irrefutable. It was an honor and a privilege to fly with them.

Prior to getting our MiGs up and running, Jim and I had both experienced substantial problems during various encounters with the FAA. Our task was to educate them about a flight realm of which most were totally unaware and our operating privileges depended on fostering good relations. We knew full well that our ability to operate these historic aircraft was certainly a privilege and not a right.

To that end, we were frequent correspondents whether by phone or by mail and shared a wealth of information to help preclude one another from duplicating mistakes or our efforts.

It occurred to both of us that if this type of networking was so helpful, it would very likely also be invaluable to the many other jet warbird operators throughout the United States and even abroad.

For the most part, jet warbird owners were viewed with a stigma of being prima donnas that had more money than sense and as such were either envied, disliked or both by the FAA. Further confounding the problem was the resistance by the other warbird operators that if the jet guys caused an issue they, too, would suffer the wrath of the FAA as their mandate came down in a broad brush stroke that included all surplus military aircraft.

About that time the keystone of our movement came along.

*Jim Robinson's MiG-21*

*Ed Schneider, Hoot Gibson, Paul Entrekin, Chuck Scott*

*Jim Robinson's MiG-15*

*MiG-15 flown by Paul Entrekin and MiG-21 flown by Hoot Gibson at Oshkosh*

Chuck Parnall was a Canadian Air Force exchange pilot who had done a tour with the U.S. Air Force in San Antonio. He married an American girl and decided to stay. He was selling cars at that time and enjoyed a partnership in a British Vampire with Rob Satterfield.

Chuck was also eager to get involved with the networking so the three of us collaborated to set up the initial meeting of what evolved into the Classic Jet Aircraft Association.

We obtained a list of every surplus military jet aircraft owner that had an airframe registered with the FAA and contacted each and every one to canvass them about a potential meeting date and location.

What followed was a subsequent gathering in Denver.

Our format was relatively informal and held at a local hotel that accommodated us with a substantial auditorium-like room. There was an overwhelming consensus that an organization would be extremely beneficial to all concerned and pooling our resources was indeed a practical idea to collectively protect our mutual interests.

It was clear that the State Department was under pressure from the FAA to increase restrictions or alleviate altogether the ability for civilians to procure the ever increasingly available supply of *foreign* surplus military turbine powered aircraft (SMTPA). Most surplus U.S. military jet aircraft had been "demilitarized" or, more accurately, mutilated into unflyable condition. Typically, the only ones available originated from foreign countries who had received them through one of the State Departments MAPs (military assistance programs).

The Experimental Aircraft Association (EAA) had, over time, developed a powerful lobby in Washington to help protect the privileges and, in some cases, rights of aircraft owners. Since surplus military aircraft fell into the category of "experimental" aircraft for registration purposes, in addition to their antique and sport aircraft branches, EAA had also formed a warbirds group. They had fought hard to eventually define "de-mil" as having only armament removed. The current battle at that time was an FAA Action Notice regarding life-limited parts. That action notice would have required owners to discard any part that was "timed-out" even though it might be unused.

We were smart enough to realize that re-inventing the wheel would be not only excessively costly but, possibly, counterproductive as well. So,

Jim, Chuck and I went to Oshkosh to meet with and obtain the counsel of Paul Poberezny.

As founder of the EAA, Paul was highly respected in FAA circles and the EAA was considered to be *the* authority with which they would partner to resolve issues regarding experimental, sport and warbird aircraft. We knew that his guidance would be invaluable but what we could not have imagined is that he would welcome us into the EAA family and under its umbrella so warmly and sincerely.

He was exceptionally personable and refreshingly humble for a man of his status within the aviation industry. Known world-wide by millions for his progressive and inclusive attitude, he treated us like family and, as anticipated, his sage advice was priceless.

From that meeting was born the Classic Jet Aircraft Association—although independent from the EAA.

The reason for that independence was that the majority of the jet warbird owners had experienced some form of exclusion at some time or other from the EAA warbird camp and there was significant mistrust. We felt that, over time, those attitudes (on both sides) would come to change when the benefits of uniting the warbird lobby was apparent to both entities. (Although it did eventually happen, sadly, it was short lived.)

About my father's age, I came to develop a (mutual) fondness for Paul. He was always positive and a joy to be around.

At one particular CJAA board of directors meeting in Oshkosh, Paul cruised up in his golf cart, asked the board to pardon his interruption and excused us both from the meeting. I was clueless as to his intentions but he had a crafty grin on his face that indicated he was up to something fun.

We pulled up to his house and when we went inside, I found that he had prepared a special memento for me to take home. In his extensive collection of aviation memorabilia, he had a rare 37mm shell (just like one of my MiG's cannons fired) which I had noticed during a previous tour of his home. We had a running joke about how much I coveted it and would be the much more appropriate owner but it was all in fun and I never expected such a thoughtful, personal gesture.

Departing Oshkosh via the Appleton, Wisconsin, airport and passing through airport security (pre 9/11), the agent inquired as to what was in the box in my carry-on luggage and it occurred to me that it would have to be X-rayed. I fully disclosed the nature of the inert shell and added that it was a gift from Paul. The agent smiled, handed me the box and off I went.

The round now sits in a proud place among my own extensive collection of aviation memorabilia.

With the guidance of our esteemed FAA mentor Bernie Geier, Jim, Chuck and I went on to carry the load for the group for the next few years being both officers and directors on the board. Jim was the financial foundation while Chuck and I (mostly Chuck) handled all of the administration.

*Paul Poberezny & Paul Entrekin*

*Original CJAA board*

Eventually Chuck went to work for Jim's museum and remained there until Jim closed it a few years later. He donated all the airplanes to the EAA museum.

It seemed that the fun had gradually eroded over time and dealing with the constant battles of totally unsubstantiated accusations with the Feds, understandably, took its toll on Jim's enthusiasm.

Chuck went with the jets to the EAA and became their director of flight operations until 1996 when he retired to travel and do some writing. Possibly the best thing that came of this association was Chuck's introduction and eventual marriage to Paul's sweet daughter, Bonnie Poberezny!

The CJAA board worked diligently to nurture the fledgling group but a small faction of malcontents craving total autonomy eventually prevailed and CJAA severed its ties with the EAA. Sadly, this prompted the resignation of all the board members, including me.

That group eventually recognized the error of their ways and cooler heads prevailed. I understand that a rejuvenation has evolved since then (no small task for an organization sometimes filled with egos often as inflated as their checkbooks) and I hold hope that those with noble goals will prevail.

Since my departure from the scene as an active airshow performer, it has been a pleasure to see others achieve relative success operating MiGs.

In addition to the success enjoyed by the late Bill Reesman, there are now only a couple of entities as ICAS members in the United States, Randy Ball (advertising 20 years experience), who has probably operated a MiG-17 longer than anyone in the airshow arena, the Black Diamond Team (formerly the Heavy Metal Jet Team) who operate some L-39s and now indicate they have added a MiG-17 or two since last year and another group, MiG Fury Fighters owned by Rick Sugden operating out of Driggs, Idaho, who appears to be maintaining a good reputation as well. I first learned of them through a fellow Delta pilot I flew with, David "Cujo" Macaluso, who was checking out in one of their two MiGs.

Also creating quite a niche for himself as Air USA is Don Kirlin in Quincy, Illinois. On 10 December, 2010, after a long, laborious effort (since 1994) to import MiG-29s from Kyrgyzstan, Kirlin finally saw the first (his) civilian owned MiG-29 fly with Fred Clifton at the controls. Kirlin, heir to the largest chain of Hallmark greeting card stores, markets his jet(s) primarily for government contracts.

Hot on his heels was John Sessions who operates the Historic Flight Foundation. On 23 January, 2011, his pilot, Doug Russell, flew the second MiG-29 flight at Everett, Washington. This aircraft came from Ukraine (another story fraught with lengthy delays and foreign deceit) and was refurbished by Morgan Aircraft Restorations.

So, 25 years after my first MiG display, the FAA indicates they have 40 or so MiGs registered but there are only approximately 20 flyable MiGs in the free world and they are still rare on the airshow circuit.

# Chapter 6
# THE *RUSSIAN*

Considering the egos that prevail among us airshow types, it should come as no surprise that we all are eager to please sponsors when asked to be featured on radio and television interviews.

Of course when you mix a performer's ego with that of a fighter pilot, you can only imagine what you'll get.

As "The Bandit" or "Mr. MiG" I thoroughly enjoyed taking full advantage of those opportunities and they were plentiful.

Using *Bandit* as a call sign was logical among my military counterparts but civilian pilots are not usually as prone to use call signs to address one another. First names normally suffice.

Early in my first airshow season I had the pleasure of flying along with some highly regarded performers, not the least of which was Leo Loudenslager. We became friends and I enjoyed the fact that he was unpretentious despite his notoriety and unparalleled skill as an aerobatic pilot. He was the first to refer to me as *Mr. MiG*.

The late Jimmy Rossi later named his MiG-17 Mr. MiG which I also took as a compliment.

What follows are some of the more interesting and memorable experiences with the media that I conveyed in my previous book, *Mighty Hands*. There are also some insights into other selected events that occurred as I left contrails across the continent throughout my 20 years flying MiGs.

While flying in Seattle at the Emerald City Flight Festival to support the new Museum of Flight, I was asked to do a live spot on a noon television talk show at KIRO. One of the hosts, Steve Raible, was going to do a quick promo for the airshow with me following an interview with actor John Davidson who was in town for a performance. The dynamics during a commercial break for a live television broadcast can be hectic with a finite amount of time to accomplish what has to be done. While one guest is departing the set, the next one has to be miked (with the cord hidden underneath clothing), seated and ready for a smooth transition in mere seconds. I had been introduced to the producer by one of the airshow folks who accompanied me to the station. Judging by the appearance of my flight suit, replete with its Soviet fighter weapons school patch, CCCP patch and a name tag with Russian wings and my name in Cyrillic letters (coupled with minimal time to prepare) she apparently assumed that I was, indeed, a *real* Russian MiG pilot. That was a relatively common mistake upon which I capitalized with relative frequency at these types of venues. It occurred to her that in all the haste she had neglected to determine the extent of my English vocabulary and whether or not an interpreter would be necessary and available. She was close to panic stricken with only seconds remaining to go on the air. Me being me, I played along briefly acknowledging her questions with only short replies in a broken accent and then, when her anxiety was nearly palpable, soothed her fears by letting her know who I truly was.

Determined to not be the only recipient of the gag, she encouraged me to continue the ruse with the hosts right up until we went live. The expressions of relief were hilarious and we enjoyed a fun interview that seemed to be well received.

A similar opportunity presented itself when I arrived at Amarillo, Texas, to stage the MiG a few days prior to their airshow. It was typical for me to depart a show site following a Sunday performance and arrive at the following weekend's venue either that same day or Monday. That afforded me the opportunity to provide some advance media coverage for the airshow and then fly home commercially (a sound business strategy that was much more cost effective than using the MiG as a conveyance) for a couple of days. Depending upon the needs on the show, I'd usually return on Thursday.

Anyway, upon my arrival at the airport, I met the show's representative who greeted me at the chocks. He asked if I had time to do an interview with the local TV station, which I did, and he gave me a quick tutorial of some talking points they hoped I would utilize. Since we were waiting for the arrival of the TV van, I suggested we lay a trap for the gullible cub reporter. He agreed and we hatched our plan.

It was easy to see that the young lady was absolutely fascinated with her opportunity to interview a *real* Russian MiG pilot. She introduced herself which I acknowledged with a slight bow and a handshake. My accomplice gave her my name and she giggled with excitement. Once the cameraman indicated he was rolling tape, she proceeded to ask her questions. Following each one, I would look directly at the gentleman standing next to me who would repeat exactly what she had said except much slower. I responded with that goofy broken accent which seemed to pique her excitement even more. At some point her naïveté became so comical that I thought I'd laugh out loud, so I finally just answered a question in plain English. She was stunned. After a brief pause, she used her microphone to bop me on the head and we all shared a good laugh. I was later told that when the interview aired it was played in its entirety at the expense of the young correspondent.

Perhaps my most enjoyable experience as *The Russian* involved a flight with my dear friend and fellow Marine, Floyd McGowin.

*General Treshchov
(the inscription reads)
"To best pilot Paul Entrekin in memoir of the Hero of the Soviet Union"*

*General Popkov  
(the inscription reads)  
"To Paul Entrekin, Pilot Gifted by God.  
Thank You for the Flight Together."*

As a patron of the Air Force Air Command & Staff College's annual "Gathering of Eagles", Floyd often hosted the notable, world renown aviators as guests at his beautiful estate in Chapman, Alabama, and sometimes took them flying in one of his airplanes. He had a beautifully restored SNJ, a Stearman, Great Lakes, Baron and a Cessna 185. His spectacular grass strip was meticulously manicured like a putting green and his hangar, replete with lithographs, prints, photos and an extraordinary library was immaculate.

During one of those visits in 1993, Floyd escorted two Russian World War II aces on a tour of the Alabama and Florida gulf coast. He suggested we rendezvous over a VOR near Montgomery on his return to Maxwell with the VIPs to give them an introduction as to what flying was like in the free world.

Air Force Lieutenant General Vitali Ivanovich Popkov and Major General Konstantin Michailovich Treshchov, both "Heroes of the Soviet Union" were 71 at the time.

I joined on Floyd's wing and flew close formation in the MiG providing these former foes with the thrill of seeing one of their old fighters now escorting them in America. The elderly gentlemen in their officer's dress uniforms literally sprinted from Floyd's Baron after we landed, eager to see the MiG-15 and wondering about the pilot who was flying it and most curious as to how.

During my early years flying the MiG back and forth across North America, not every destination afforded such an amiable greeting.

Here are a couple that began with some hostility.

At a fuel stop in Martinsburg, West Virginia, which, at the time, was a small joint-use facility shared by Air Force transport aircraft, I was greeted by automatic weapons trained at the MiG and me.

While on final for a visual approach, the tower controller (no doubt looking at me through his binoculars and seeing 3 cannon barrels extended from the nose and a couple of drop tanks that could easily be confused for bombs) asked me to re-confirm my type of aircraft. I confirmed it was a MiG and he cleared me to land. What thoughts went through his head are anyone's guess but he obviously felt concerned enough to contact Air Force security personnel who quickly rolled their MPs.

After switching to ground control I was cleared to taxi to the civilian ramp. Before I had shut down the engine a blue government pickup truck with sirens blaring and lights flashing screeched to a stop nose to nose with the jet. The MPs pointed their rifles toward the cockpit and were shouting something which I couldn't really hear. I finished my post-landing checklist and secured the engine. When I took off my helmet I clearly heard "Identify yourself!" I calmly (at least as calmly as one can with M-16s trained on them) waved and said "How y'all doin'?" As they eased from behind the safety of their truck doors I overheard one say "He ain't no Russian." Thankfully, they lowered their guns and walked over to the jet where I explained who I was. We all shared a laugh at the expense of the vivid imagination of the controller who had somehow convinced himself that perhaps the Russians were invading West Virginia.

And then there was the airport security cop who was right out of a TV reality show that could be called "Bayou Buffoons".

Upon arrival at the Shreveport, Louisiana, airport, I was directed into a parking spot on their transient ramp by a line boy. Once again, following what must be standard security protocol, a cruiser (blue lights flashing) pulled in front of the jet as I secured the engine and hopped off the wing.

This diminutive guy who couldn't have weighed more than a buck thirty five dripping wet, conjured up his best scowl, propped his hand on what looked like maybe a .357 revolver and commanded "Lemme see 'at driver's license boy"!

I managed to subdue a grin as I watched the personification of Barney Fife and respectfully indicated that I would gladly show it to him just as soon as I retrieved my wallet from under my G suit which, of course, I needed to do inside at the rest room. He agreed to wait so I opened the fuel caps and gave the line boy fueling instructions before heading into the FBO. At the service desk, I was informed that the old antagonist was a harmless but daily problem and that they would take care of his concerns. They radioed the line boy to tell Barney to move his car for incoming aircraft and he dutifully complied. Then, he cautiously observed (with one hand on his pistol at all times) as I strapped in, cranked the engine and slowly pulled away from the ramp. His chance to bust what just *must* have been a Russian bad guy had just evaporated.

I wondered, after that, if he had any bullets in that pistol or maybe just one in his pocket.

I've met some of the most famous aviators, truly living legends, due to doors being opened by the MiG.

Probably my favorite is the incomparable Bob Hoover.

Having just completed my Saturday performance at the Oklahoma City airshow, I took advantage of the wonderful accommodations the sponsors provided to help us cope with the 100+ degree heat. There was a large air-conditioned motor home near the flight line that contained water, soft drinks and light snacks as well as comfortable places to sit and relax. I was surprised to see that the only other person inside was Mr. Hoover. He looked quite refreshed in his flight suit with his big Panama hat sitting on the table. With eyes that squinted through his thick glasses and a big smile that welcomed me he said, "Come on in young fella. Nice show!" I figured he was just being nice but truly appreciated his comment more than he could possibly have known.

I couldn't help noticing that he maintained a Cheshire cat grin as he watched me grab a Coke and plop down in a soft chair. I gulped a swallow or two and wondered what was up. Finally, he said "I've got some good news for you. My good friend, Bob Goodrich, is the Director of Flight Standards for the FAA and he called me with some concerns about some fella flying the circuit with a MiG. Since I told him we'd be performing together here, he asked me to do an informal evaluation on you and I'm happy to say you passed with flying colors! I like the way you use the jet's energy. It reminds me of the way I flew the Sabre."

Well, how about that?

I had just unknowingly received a check ride from Mr. Energy Management himself . . . and passed with praise!

Other than a very astute eye, how could he possibly have known that my technique, like his, was to set power on the engine and leave it alone throughout the routine, trading altitude for airspeed or vice versa. If you ever saw him fly his Shrike Commander or P-51 routine you, like me, were in awe of his skill.

Following that encounter, I would occasionally see him at airshows or other functions including the ICAS convention in Las Vegas each December. He graciously put his arm around *his protégé* and we'd swap stories about the preceding season.

Chuck Yeager called Bob Hoover the best pilot he ever saw.

And yes, I have good Chuck Yeager story, too.

I mentioned in the introduction that prior to my first flight in the MiG-15 I received some "guidance" from General Yeager. I had read his autobiography (published in 1985—shortly before I acquired my MiG) and was intrigued, in particular, with what he wrote in the chapter titled Outflying the Russians. He said "Flying the MiG is the most demanding situation I have ever faced. It's a quirky airplane that's killed a lot of its pilots."

Those who know me and have heard me wax eloquent about my few encounters with "the world's greatest battery salesman" are aware that he's not one of my favorite people. I've said many times that his legitimate accomplishments in aviation certainly merit many of the accolades he has received. Unfortunately, though, he has not been content to ride the wave of notoriety received from those accomplishments alone. Instead he seems to have a penchant for not only embellishing his own achievements but also belittling those of others. With very few exceptions he is unabashedly uncomplimentary of his contemporaries (in his mind he has very few peers) and has gone out of his way in his writings to speak poorly of such aviation icons as Neil Armstrong and many other astronauts and test pilots.

Not knowing this about him at the time, though, I managed to locate his phone number simply by calling directory assistance in Grass Valley, California, where he lived with his wife Glennis at the time.

Except for the recent publication of his book (ghost written primarily by Leo Janis) he had lapsed pretty much into obscurity by that time having ridden the wave of notoriety until it fizzled out years before. Soon to follow, though, was his resurgence of celebrity after an AC Delco battery commercial which, once again, returned him to prominence.

He clung desperately to the persona of a test pilot attempting to convince anyone who still held him in high regard and would hang on his every word as he held court at various Air Force receptions to which he was invited from time to time that he was still the best.

Anyway, I got his number, phoned his house and after passing the filter of his wife's discernment proceeded to explain who I was and what I needed. Somewhere in the process, though, something was lost in translation.

I had just explained that the jet was in Chino, California, when he came unglued and let go with an expletive laced tirade that made a couple of references to Ed Maloney which made absolutely no sense to me. (I later learned that the Planes of Fame Museum, operated by Maloney, had, according to Yeager, reneged on an opportunity for him to fly one of their Mustangs due to insurance issues and that had really made him mad.) Yeager assumed that Maloney had acquired the MiG and somehow wanted his involvement in the flight test process. He made an interesting comment that I never forgot . . . "I can fly a damn MiG any time I want to!"

When he finally took a breath I was able to convey that I had no affiliation with Maloney and reaffirm the reason for my call. Only then did he offer a couple of words of advice. (See page 12.)

Years later, after I conveyed this story to a mutual friend of ours, Ed Bowlin, who was a Delta pilot (along with his lovely wife Connie) and well known for operating his & her Mustangs, Ed arranged for Yeager and me to meet at Maxwell Air Force Base where I would bring the MiG as a static display for the Air Command and Staff College's annual Gathering of Eagles. Yeager was to be one of the honorees.

With Ed's introduction and light hearted recollection of my story, Yeager warmed up during that weekend and was actually quite cordial, especially over a couple of cocktails which he enjoyed profusely.

*Paul Entrekin & Chuck Yeager*

*Two MiG Pilots*

Eventually he wanted to climb into the cockpit (which I gladly obliged) and he proceeded to point out, with some error, the meaning of various switches and gauges. I couldn't fault memories of 40 years prior so I just smiled and nodded affirmatively.

While I have enjoyed the persona of being *The Russian*, I have even more enjoyed making the acquaintance of a few real Russians that I've been most fortunate to encounter.

In addition to the two WW II Russian aces mentioned previously, I was also privileged to meet and become friends with Viktor Belenko.

According to Viktor, the account of his defection is only relatively accurate in John Barron's book, *MiG PILOT—The Final Escape of Lieutenant Belenko*.

Understandably, he is a very private person with the specter of the old KGB still looming. Among the first to defect from the old Soviet Union, he gave them a big black eye which, it is cautiously presumed, some would very much still like to avenge.

On 6 September, 1976, Viktor left his base in Chuguyevka and flew a 7 month old MiG-25 interceptor (NATO code named Foxbat) to Hakodate, Japan. The jet was capable of Mach 3+ and over 100,000 feet so, with CIA U-2 and SR-71 intelligence gathering flights actively ongoing, western intelligence agencies were eager to learn of its capabilities and limitations.

At 29 years old, disenchanted with the façade of communism and faced with the grim prospects of a life within the "abusive, wicked Soviet regime", like the North Korean, Ken Rowe, Viktor's flight to freedom was undertaken with a cumulative desire for a new life. He said "I compare my escape with the American immigrants who left/escaped from their old countries . . . I left that country with class."

Viktor had trained in the L-29 and instructed in the MiG-17 and SU-15 before his assignment in the MiG-25.

Of particular interest to me was his recollection of being taught as a student pilot "If a MiG-17 ever goes into a spin, eject at once. You can pull it out of a spin but it's hard." And he told me he related to *his* students "If you are stupid enough to get yourself into a spin, most likely, you are not smart enough to recover from it. Moreover, you are not born to fly fighters and your place is in a flying barn*. Spins have no tactical value. It is abuse of the airframe and pilots head."

(*Viktor elaborated; "Flying barn is any big aircraft with more than one ejection seat . . . those which were flown by a committee.)

He was exceptionally skilled, proven by his ability to get his jet to Japan; landing with what he approximated was 30 seconds of fuel remaining.

Another issue of concern was always in the back of my mind, particularly when flying a MiG-15 UTI.

I was aware that renowned Russian cosmonaut Yuri Gagarin, the first man in space (12 April, 1961), had died in a MiG-15 UTI mishap on 27 March, 1968. He was 34 years old. The circumstances surrounding that crash were disputed and therefore inconclusive. So, I wondered; if such an esteemed pilot (and his instructor) could be caught unaware, how would *I* overcome a seemingly insurmountable abnormal in-flight emergency? It was a sobering thought.

Once incorporated into American society and the U.S. government aerospace industry, Viktor proved to be invaluable as a consultant for soviet tactics.

He was given access to a secret facility that housed flight simulators for the MiG-17, MiG-21, MiG-23 and MiG-25 where he enlightened our engineers as to the real capabilities of the aircraft versus what had been programmed.

The insight he provided amounted to an intelligence coup and, as such, was unprecedented.

Although he has worked in real estate development, commercial fishing in Alaska, diesel automotive service, investment banking and spoken at Soviet reality seminars for various U.S. government groups, when asked what he wanted to do after he'd been here for a while, his reply was simple—he wanted to be a Montana cowboy.

Then, in 1993, I met and became friends with Alexander Zuyev.

As chronicled in his book *FULCRUM—A Top Gun Pilot's Escape from the Soviet Empire* (with Malcolm McConnell), at 28 years old he flew a MiG-29 from "Ruslan" air base near Mikha Tskhakaya (formerly the city of Senaki) in western Georgia to Trabzon, Turkey, on 20 May, 1989.

The account of his defection experience included a gunfight with an enlisted ramp guard. Both he and the guard managed to shoot each other at close range but both recovered.

Much like Viktor and Ken Rowe, he was disenchanted with the throes of communism and due to the politics surrounding an ugly potential divorce, his life as a Soviet Air Force pilot was essentially over. Following the Tbilisi massacre of political demonstrators, Alex finally made his decision to leave the USSR.

Alex had also trained in the L-29 and had flown the MiG-23 Flogger, an F-14 Tomcat-like, variable-geometry, "swing wing" Mach 2+ fighter.

And, like Viktor Belenko, he was a tremendous intelligence asset regarding current Soviet tactics and equipment.

Following his DOD consulting in the 1991 gulf war, in the spirit of perestroika his family (mother and siblings) was granted exit visas and came to join him in the United States. He lived to see the fall of the USSR later that year.

Sadly, in 2001 Alex was killed (ironically) in a Yak-52 crash while riding with the owner.

He wanted to be an airline pilot.

While I never had the opportunity to fly with either Alex or Viktor, I did get to fly a series of formation flights with a Ukrainian MiG-29 demonstration team during their North American tour in July of 1992.

Chief Pilot Captain Nikolai Koval and I briefed through an interpreter on the ground but, except for some very simple, agreed upon English and Russian phrases, I could not communicate with him and the other pilot once airborne so it was imperative that we stick to our scripted routine precisely.

Although we only flew some very elementary formation photo passes at the Minot Air Force Base airshow in North Dakota, the experience was enormously fun. The constant chatter between the two MiG-29s joining on my wings was, at times, surreal.

*Paul Entrekin & Alex Zuyev*

*Paul Entrekin & Ukranian MiG-29 Team*

# Chapter 7
# KARMA

Every pilot has a "there I was" story.

Some of us have more than others and that's not necessarily because we have more flight time, more experience or more vivid imaginations. In some cases it's because we've done some dumb things in airplanes and just happen to be fortunate enough to have survived our own stupidity. In all fairness, too, sometimes things just happen despite the best intentions, planning and skill. We all know somebody who got dead or severely injured or hurt someone else because of an aircraft mishap.

I consider myself blessed, not lucky.

As a young Marine pilot I came very close to smashing a Huey into a cliff on Okinawa attempting to maintain VFR in rapidly deteriorating weather conditions.

Through no particular skill of my own but, rather, divine intervention, I managed to save myself, my crew and my passengers.

While doing aerobatics in my Pitts S-2B I experienced a clogged fuel filter that caused an engine failure. When my first option, an attempted re-start, failed and since I was flying over water, I quickly eliminated my second option of bailing out. That left me the challenge of attempting to glide (at 1200 feet AGL) a distance I doubted possible into an area where I was guessing the location of a runway obscured at that altitude by pine trees. I was highly motivated to not hit those tress and, again, by the grace of God managed to *land* on the runway. It wasn't pretty because in the process of stretching the glide as far as possible I had to nearly stall the Pitts to clear the last of the trees prior to the runway clearing. I touched down on asphalt and stayed on asphalt even though I landed *perpendicular* on that runway. Both main tires were flattened and the wheel pants were dinged when the bungees flexed but, thankfully, I didn't ding the prop and, even more thankfully didn't flip.

Anybody in the cockpit that day would definitely agree that a Higher Power interceded.

One other close call that merits mention involved an anomaly I experienced in the BD-5J.

While participating in a DOD contract using BD-5Js to simulate the radar profile of the Chinese "Seersucker" cruise missile, I was flying a routine mission when I noticed that my wing fuel was not transferring properly. Since I was halfway to my destination and calculated that I would have adequate fuel to get there, I elected to continue. At altitude I adjusted power settings to determine that I could fly an acceptable approach speed even with one wing full and the other near empty. I set up for a long final and maintained a slightly higher than normal airspeed.

*Paul Entrekin & BD-5J Bud Light Microjet*

Once over the threshold, I reduced power at about 10 feet and began a slight flare. With no warning, the left wing stalled and dropped uncontrollably. I attempted to compensate by pushing the side-stick control all the way to the right but the jet hit the runway hard on the left wing and I skidded off the left side of the runway into the grass.

Had I reduced power on final to set airspeed for a normal approach, I now know that the jet would very likely have stalled as it did over the runway resulting in an unsurvivable crash. As it was, damage was minimal and I was unscathed.

The jet flew again up until four years later when another pilot experienced an unknown anomaly and lost his life in the crash.

And of course, like most pilots, there are other incidents that served to eventually make me a much better and safer pilot.

I'm very fortunate to have never experienced an abnormal or emergency in an airliner that so much as raised my blood pressure.

Without a doubt, though, the closest I ever came to becoming a statistic occurred at the Robins Air Force Base airshow in Macon, Georgia.

It was spring time and the sweet, redolent scent of peach blossoms permeated the air. The weather was gorgeous; not too hot, a gentle breeze and relatively low humidity following a frontal passage.

During that time period, I was keeping the MiG at a hangar at Charlie Brown Airport in Atlanta with Earl Arrowood, one of my good friends at Delta who had started a business called Sky Warriors. He had some excellent pilots that would take paying customers up for a T-34 dogfight. There were thoughts of how to incorporate a MiG into the business as an adversary aircraft and we were still in the planning stages of that potential deal.

During a lull between airshows, I decided to finally replace the attitude gyro in the jet.

Having flown with the not necessarily archaic but odd, none the less, stock Russian attitude gyro and compass (previously mentioned in the introduction) for several years, I finally decided that zipping around the friendly skies partial panel during IMC conditions would eventually catch up with me. Besides, the single-pilot work load was busy enough without having to think backwards and upside down.

For inexplicable reasons, the Russians had determined that an attitude gyro should have the sky reference on the bottom of the instrument and the ground reference on the top. So, their gyros were blue on the bottom and brown on the top. Imagine rolling inverted and that's what these gyros looked like in normal flight. Here's what really made it weird. Pulling *aft* on the stick to climb would cause the aircraft index (pipper) to go *down* into the (blue) sky. Conversely, the index indication of pushing *forward* on the stick was seeing the pipper go *up* towards the (brown) ground.

After years of flying in actual instrument conditions and being accustomed to seeing a specific indication correspond to a control input, you can imagine how bizarre it was to see the opposite of what your brain anticipated.

When I could not avoid IMC conditions, I improvised, adapted and overcame that problem by disregarding the gyro altogether and using the VSI and turn needle—partial panel.

Fortunately, the bank angle indicator on the gyro did, at least, correspond to the direction of turn.

The directional gyro was substantially easier to comprehend. It had a fixed but adjustable compass card with an airplane index in the center which rotated to point to the compass direction corresponding to the flight path. For example, with the compass card adjusted so that north was at twelve o'clock and you were traveling east, the airplane index would be pointed to 090 degrees at three o'clock. While it was more user friendly than the attitude gyro, it was screwy none the less.

So here's what happened.

The avionics technician I hired was recommended by another trusted pilot so I had confidence that he was capable. Even though he was well regarded, he was very, very slow and full of excuses for the delays. I had missed two airshows because of his failure to have the jet finished when promised and I was adamant about not missing the Robins show, too. After persistent prodding on my part, he finally completed the job and I was pleasantly surprised when I saw the instrument panel. He reconfigured it slightly to accommodate the new instrumentation and it looked really good.

I flew the short, uneventful flight from Atlanta to Macon the next day.

During the first day's performance I had just finished a maneuver and was doing a tuck under roll reversal to reposition. Heading south and 3/8s through the roll at about 200 feet AGL and 300 knots, an audible "pop" inside the cockpit got my attention. One of nuts on the four large thumb screws that held the center instrument panel in place had backed off under pressure. The panel had been misaligned and forced into position with the instruments improperly seated. Obviously in a hurry to get the job done, the technician had not checked the nuts for proper tightness so normal aircraft vibration and G loading eventually caused all the nuts to loosen.

The distraction brought my attention from outside the cockpit (where it should have been) to inside where I quickly deduced that the panel might either fall into my lap or on my legs and feet. Had that happened, I would most likely have lost control of the aircraft.

The decision making process took, perhaps, a millisecond.

I reacted to the sound and sight of what was happening by reaching with my left hand to stop further potential panel movement. With the stick in my right hand already at full deflection for the roll (stay with me here), the motion of my left arm pushing forward on the panel rotated my shoulders enough to cause my right arm to pull slightly aft.

This all occurred in the time it took for the jet to complete another 2/8s of the roll so I was then nearly inverted.

My first reaction was instinctive. The next one was decisive.

I had two choices—either stop the roll and push forward on the stick to climb out inverted with negative G or continue the momentum with a rolling pull out. Again, relying on instinct, most pilots (as I did) would probably choose the more comfortable positive G maneuver and pull. In hindsight, having re-lived the incident countless times in my dreams, I probably should have taken the shortest distance to recover and pushed. Then again, who knows what the damned panel would have done under negative G conditions?

Either way, I knew it would be close.

Everything from that point to climbing safely away from terra firma seemed to be in slow motion as I tried desperately to *will* the MiG to roll faster. Once past 90 degrees angle of bank (three quarters of the way through the roll) I pulled as hard as I could but the leaves on the trees below were still getting closer and I subconsciously determined that I probably wouldn't make it. It was surprisingly serene to know that I'd done all I could as I waited for the inevitable impact.

What followed was a surreal sensation that I was still very much alive, flying and extremely puzzled as to how and why.

It was fortuitous that the terrain was rolling away from my flight path and I somehow followed that contour until reaching a positive rate of climb. I was later told that, from the crowd's perspective, I actually disappeared from view.

I deduced that the panel had probably moved as much as it would and everything was back under control.

I completed the show with a simple photo pass, landed and taxied toward the parking ramp with adrenaline still surging in my system. After I secured the engine and removed my helmet, I sat momentarily in the cockpit and looked again at the panel where I noticed the G meter pegged just past the 10 positive G limit on the accelerometer.

Whether you are inclined toward things spiritual or not, I can state unequivocally that I have no doubt I am alive today following these significant aeronautical experiences because of divine intervention. It certainly wasn't because of luck or my skill. I believe it was *the Master's* skill guiding my hands with His own and His will that there was more for me to do with this lifetime.

# Chapter 8
# World Records

As previously mentioned, I had earned my wings of gold as a fledgling naval aviator at NAS Whiting Field near Pensacola in 1980 and later served as a flight instructor there with the memories of my experiences still fresh and vivid.

I had a fondness for Whiting because of the significance it played in my flying career so I was glad to be invited to perform at the airshow which would celebrate their 50th anniversary.

Airshow performers are usually quite agreeable to doing whatever they can to help their sponsors with publicity and promotion and I wanted to provide something special in association with a place I held dear. So, I contacted the National Aeronautic Association to request a sanction to set a speed record. (The NAA is the recognized governing body in this country for *national* record-making aviation and space events. They further oversee the documentation of *world* records claimed in conjunction with those flights for the Federation Aéronautique Internationale or FAI. Records are defined by a class and category for different types of aircraft.)

Once the necessary paperwork was completed and the sanction for the attempt was granted, on July 6, 1993, I flew from Atlanta to Pensacola in 25 minutes and 30 seconds establishing a "speed over a recognized course" national and world record in the MiG-15. Whiting tower mistakenly reported my *touchdown* time rather than the time I crossed the tower which extended the "official" time by five minutes. Even so, the record was in excess of 500 miles per hour.

ATC granted me a straight out departure on course and directly to 10,000 feet. I could have shortened the record time substantially by taking off and doing an air start after a turn in the pattern to build speed. (Because of the sanction for a speed record attempt I was waivered to exceed 250 knots below 10,000 feet.) However, since weight was a factor in achieving the maximum speed possible, I had calculated a minimum fuel load for a burn that did not include the turn in the pattern.

With no air conditioning and only minimal ambient vent air, the temperature in the cockpit was close to 120 degrees for the entire flight.

That didn't seem to bother the little MiG, though. It flew like a banshee with rock solid engine performance that told me it wanted the record as much as I. By that time, with more than a thousand hours together, we could feel each other's subtle idiosyncrasies and discern by feel and sound what the other wanted. We had become melded partners.

My next opportunity to set records had nothing to do with the MiG.

It was also in conjunction, though, with a very special occasion—the final Delta Air Lines passenger flight sequence of the venerable Boeing 727.

As one of the three most senior First Officers on the 727, I was fortunate to be scheduled to fly with Captain Bob Falkins and Second Officer Kellie Waddell on the jet's final rotation.

I hatched the idea of the record attempt and Bob ran it up the flag pole at the Delta corporate offices. They bought into the idea and I was tasked with applying for the sanction.

The last pairing would be a simple out and back from Atlanta to Greensboro, North Carolina and since Bob chose to fly the final leg and make the last scheduled 727 landing with passengers, I was afforded the honor of being at the controls for the record attempt.

So, on April 6, 2003, we flew the route in 37 minutes averaging 486 miles per hour. After some photographs and a brief celebration with a large cake commemorating the event, we boarded our Atlanta bound passengers on flight 607, swapped second officers so that the most senior engineer, Leo Coffield, could occupy the panel and flew our jet into the annals of airline history.

# Chapter 9
# THE AIRSHOW POLITICOS

Eventually, as somewhat of a groundbreaking airshow performer in the jet warbird community, I came to garner a modicum of respect within the industry's preeminent organization, ICAS—the International Council of Air Shows.

I was nominated for and accepted a two year term that involved representing the jet warbird performers regarding individual and group safety issues on what was then known as the Performer Safety Committee (now the Aerobatic Competency Evaluator or ACE Committee).

We were small in number but had the backing of the FAA to recommend changes in performer status such as lowering authorized performance altitudes as low as ground level. It was a serious and sobering responsibility.

While it was awesome to be the first MiG pilot flying airshows across North America and thrilling to experience significant other aviation firsts, of all my contributions to the airshow industry, this is the one of which I am most proud.

As an example of the issues we faced, there's a commonly circulated photo and video on the internet that occasionally is attributed to me. I'm glad to say, I am *not* the pilot flying in that particular photo or video.

It is a truly incredible sequence flown by the late Doug Shultz.

Doug was one of the few pilots able to claim to have tied the low altitude record and lived to tell the tale.

Flying his MiG-17 at an airshow in Harrison, Arkansas, Doug later explained to me that, during his aerobatic routine, he felt he was "a little low" at the top of a loop so he spontaneously concluded that it would be a good idea to extend his flaps to 15 (takeoff position). How he justified the hypothesis that he would somehow shorten the radius of his loop with flaps extended was never made clear.

It *didn't* shorten the radius of the loop and he impacted terra firma (grass) during his recovery at the bottom, dragging the engine exhaust can along the ground. He climbed out of that near disaster and managed to land on the runway.

To further complicate Doug's lapse in judgment, only a cursory external visual inspection was undertaken and the jet was flown back to its home base. Subsequent internal inspection revealed that there was, in fact, significant damage.

Doug was well regarded due to his prior experience as a graduate of the Navy's Fighter Weapons School (Top Gun) and his experience as a captain with Delta Air Lines. Although small in stature, he displayed the characteristic stereotypical fighter pilot cockiness and had an arrogance that made it sometimes difficult to tell him anything critical.

I later observed him flying recklessly in a MiG-21 at an airshow in Jackson, Mississippi. The FAA inspector on sight was furious after a couple of very low passes too close to the crowd. Another pilot and I assured the inspector that we would discuss the issue with Doug so as to preclude him from losing his license on the spot—the result of which would have been catastrophic for his airline career. Although he acknowledged his indiscretion and indicated he would not repeat it the following day, he did. Certificate action initiated by the FAA was pending but Doug slipped away before the inspector could notify him personally.

A few weeks later, Doug was killed in the MiG-21 when it apparently disintegrated during a high speed flight over water near the west coast of Canada.

He was flying in conjunction with a government contract that called for supersonic flight, possibly as high as Mach 2. Only a few parts of the aircraft were located.

Several years later I was approached to fly a MiG-17 owned by Curt Farley, a retired airline pilot. Since the MiG-15 and MiG-17 are so significantly similar, the letter of authorization (in lieu of a type rating) pilots receive is usually for the MiG-15/17 series. I originally received only a MiG-15 LOA but following an endorsement from John Penney, I had the MiG-17 added.

In addition to offering the bright red Fresco as a solo, Curt also owned a Venom that had been in service with the Swiss and was marketing both jets as a dog fight act.

He kept the planes in his hangar facility at the Culpeper, Virginia, airport and ran his operation as a hobby on a shoestring budget. He hoped that my name would lend some credibility to his efforts and allow him to grow his market area from a regional to a national scale.

I enjoyed flying the jet for solo aerobatic demonstrations and was able to fly it supersonic a couple of times.

I did *not*, however, enjoy the dual routines with Curt. He was dangerous and in addition to the attention necessary for a safe, low level aerobatic demonstration, I had to have my head on a constant swivel to avoid mid-air collisions with him.

He was hard-headed, especially when it came to criticism of his own capabilities. Although he had also flown large aircraft as an Air Force pilot, he was out of his element in single seat fighter or attack jets. He frequently lost situational awareness during our numerous practice flights in an aerobatic box and "knock it off" calls were far too commonplace. During de-briefings I tried diligently to bring him up to speed but he appeared to be incapable of consistently incorporating the necessary changes to his attitude and skill level.

After a couple of years, those "knock it off" calls became excessive at actual airshow sites so I gave Curt notice that the current season would be my last. I did help him bring another qualified pilot in to replace me and, since Curt decided to then become the primary MiG pilot, helped the new guy with an aerobatic competency check in the Venom.

Perhaps the act eventually fizzled into anonymity which, in hindsight, was a better alternative than blazing into a smoking hole.

That high profile exposure on the Performer Safety Committee coupled with the fact that for three years I was a full time airshow performer, made it substantially easier to get to know many of the others who made their primary living within the airshow business.

Prior to that time, as a "newbie" in the industry, I was a naive businessman, unsuspecting of the ruthlessness that could prevail among perceived competitors. I learned my lessons well and quickly.

Initially I rode the coattails of Byrd Mapoles, "the Flying Mayor of Milton", who graciously allowed me to accompany him at my first ICAS convention in 1986. Milton is close to Pensacola and having seen Byrd perform over the years I had a great respect for his abilities as a pilot and knew I could glean significant knowledge from his experience. He was reluctant to encourage me but agreed to be somewhat of a mentor when he realized I was pressing on with or without his guidance. He was instrumental in introducing me to various show sponsors which helped me get a running start my first season.

There were certain other individuals in the warbird community, though, who were determined to dissuade me from entering what they perceived to be *their* exclusive domain and I was told (in vain) that they had "crunched the numbers" and conclusively determined that operating a jet could not be viable in the airshow arena. The foremost of that ilk were Frank Sanders and Rick Brickert.

Sanders flew the number 4 Team America SIAI Marchetti. He had a warbird restoration and maintenance business in Chino where he had renovated and modified a Hawker Sea Fury for racing. He became noteworthy for marketing a wing tip or missile rail mounted smoke generating system which he called the "Sanders Smokewinder"—a play on the sidewinder missile name. With a history primarily as a mechanic, he was considered a good pilot but not necessarily known for exceptional flying abilities.

He also enjoyed some notoriety for a paper he published emphasizing pilot stress. Although, to my knowledge, he did not have substantive formal education in either subject, his missive contained references to both the psychology and physiology of flying. One must presume his perspective came primarily from his own experiences.

Regardless of the accuracy of what he conveyed, he was convincing enough with his assimilation of the information to make his point, right or wrong. And that was the essence of my issue with Frank Sanders.

He seemed to consider himself a preeminent airshow pilot and, in my experience, wary of anyone who might question or expose his views as erroneous or, even worse, overshadow what he perceived to be his turf.

Before my time, Frank was apparently perceived as somewhat of a safety guru within the relatively small cadre of west coast warbird pilots.

I later learned that Frank was vocal and highly critical of the fact that I had flown helicopters as a naval aviator but he was totally unaware that I had more fixed wing than rotary wing flight time and, further, had no idea of my actual skill or experience.

After my displaying the MiG on the airshow circuit in 1987, Frank made it a point to ask proprietary questions about the logistics and support that contributed to my success that year and, being the naive young businessman that I was, I unsuspectingly obliged by revealing the keys to that success. Within months, Sanders had teamed up with Rick Brickert and had readied a T-33 they called the Red Knight.

Initially I wasn't concerned because there were so few jet warbirds available nationally and I believed there were plenty of airshows to go around. Marketing and touting their act on its own merits was only a part of their strategy, though.

I would soon learn how vicious business competition could be.

At the 1988 ICAS convention, Frank had taken advantage of an opportunity during a seminar to warn all who would listen about "a very unsafe pilot who was trying to do airshows in a MiG". Even though he cautiously did not mention me by name, because of my notoriety and the fact that there were only a couple of others who had acquired MiGs by then, most in attendance assumed his comments were about me and the negative connotation soon spread.

After three days of only sparse visits to my booth at the convention, I was pondering why there were so few bookings coming in. The publicity I received was tremendous and the MiG and I were hailed worldwide. All the acclaim was positive and the free world's first MiG flight display was hot. Finally, a guy from the Point Mugu airshow stopped to talk and provided the insight about what Frank had said and, more importantly, the pejorative way in which he had said it. Although when I confronted him later Frank told me he was referring to a different guy who was flailing around the west coast, scaring the hell out of himself, he made no attempt to clarify who he *wasn't* talking about. He backpedaled faster than a Michael Jackson moon walk realizing that he might have exposed himself to some serious liability.

Toward the end of the convention with the damage already done, when the ICAS executive director, Rick Nadeau, was informed of Sander's antics he offered a disclaimer during the general meeting that clarified the "misunderstanding" and I managed to salvage the season with plenty of bookings.

In a touch of irony, at an airshow site in the southwest, Frank ended up killing both himself and a passenger during a media ride in the two-seat T-33 Red Knight jet. Post crash analysis indicated that, due to an attempted low level recovery, the aircraft was over stressed to the point that an aileron actually departed the jet.

Rick Brickert and I had met a year or so prior when we were both chosen to be part of a select FAA panel (the Warbird Technical Advisory Committee, chaired by Ed Bowlin) to assist them in determining the practicality of certain potential rules and regulations surrounding the surplus military aircraft currently in use.

Having been what is commonly referred to in Air Force parlance as a "guard baby", he had flown with the reserves and also was a pilot for Western Airlines based in Salt Lake City. He had wisely made himself available to fly other folk's warbird airplanes and had substantial experience. Although he had a reputation for being cocky and brash around some people, he reigned in his arrogance with those he considered his peers and we got along just fine.

Brickert managed to finally acquire another T-33 after Sanders' crash and kept the Red Knight act going. Not long after Sanders' death, though, Brickert debuted the Pond Racer at the Reno Air Races. An experimental aircraft created for the sole purpose of eventually replacing the aging warbird race planes, it was made of composite materials and sported two Nissan automobile engines. Bob Pond, the aircraft's namesake and owner of the Planes of Fame Museum in Minnesota, had funded the project.

During a race, Brickert maydayed that he was experiencing a problem and properly departed the race course according to the rules. It appeared that he had a fire onboard and attempted to land on the desert floor. Although he had an oxygen system, he either removed his mask or wasn't using it and was overcome by smoke and/or toxic fumes.

The result was fatal.

Accepting that imitation is truly the sincerest form of flattery, only one other performer (that I know of) ever replicated any of my marketing strategies or in any way infringed on my non-copyrighted persona.

Bill Reesman was an excellent strategist and got onboard the Red Bull marketing miracle early in their U.S. blitz. Bill's MiG-17 was very popular for a few years but, initially, I was told by some that he and I were thought to be working together due to the fact that he copied my flight suit right down to the same Russian patches. Once fully sponsored by Red Bull, that tactic was no longer necessary for him and he enjoyed a prosperous airshow career until his death from cancer a few years ago.

I met T. J. Brown on the airshow circuit and he eventually became the president of ICAS.

He flew the lead position in a Pitts 4-ship act known as the Holiday Inn/Coca Cola Aerobatic team. Two of his three wingmen, Mike VanWagenen and Buzz Lynch, were also former Air Force pilots and, like T. J., had test pilot backgrounds so they were intrigued with my success in the MiG.

So, it was seemingly natural that someone of T. J.'s marketing acumen would come up with the idea of operating a jet team. And what better concept to begin with than putting a MiG-15 and F-68 Sabre act together? We discussed the potential over a brief period time as we met periodically at different show sites. It was clear that we all got along well and were like-minded in our approach to showmanship, safety and professionalism.

Based in Fernandina Beach, Florida, their operation was in the same geographic area as a chain of Taco Bell franchises owned and operated around Jacksonville by Jim Gregory. T. J. and Jim were friends and became partners when they located and purchased their F-86.

Jim was very personable and friendly. I liked him right away.

With a Navy background, he had no trouble in the work-up flights that he and T. J. flew together working out the minor maintenance gripes on the Sabre and getting familiar with low level aerobatics. T. J. and I choreographed what we felt would be an entertaining dogfight and formation aerobatic sequence and spent significant time polishing the routine. The timing was very precise so as to keep a jet in front of the crowd at all times.

Solo, low level aerobatics is taxing and demanding enough but flying two first generation fighters in close proximity complicated the safety factors exponentially. It was unequivocally imperative that we hit critical corresponding geographic points in space at precise times and intervals so as to not conflict with each other. Maintaining visual contact with each other for as long as possible was critical as well.

The only other act I ever saw that did a superior job of flying this way was Jim Franklin and Eliot Cross in their Dueling Wacos act. With Johnny Kazian narrating, it was phenomenal.

With Jim and T. J.'s investment in another jet and our collective investment in jet fuel, we practiced and polished an outstanding routine. I checked T. J. out in the MiG so he was qualified in both aircraft. Jim would be the primary Sabre pilot and I would be the primary pilot for the MiG with T. J. backing us up in case either Jim or I got sick or had a scheduling conflict for a show.

T. J.'s strategy was to ensure that the dogfight act was booked along with the Pitts team so we would be at the same show sites together. His goal was to create a one stop shopping opportunity for show sponsors and he envisioned a glider act as well as, eventually, a jet team of L-39s. He even had ideas for a comedy act that would involve a cool little Fokker Tri-plane replica that he owned.

With an accountant background, his real forte was an ability to convince major sponsorship to back his ideas. His coup of attaining sponsorship from both Holiday Inn and Coca Cola was indicative of his vision and persuasive ability.

I had hitched my wagon to what was clearly a rising star within the airshow industry.

The chemistry was probably the best asset of our merger.

Everybody liked each other. The approach to the serious side of our profession was uncompromising. While there was plenty of comic relief to ease the tension of critical situations, safety for ourselves and our audiences was always paramount.

Some years later, I bumped into a former flight student from my days as an instructor at VT-3 in Pensacola. Ken "Thumper" Switzer approached me at the Tri-Cities Airshow in Tennessee and reminded me of our flying together. I expressed that I must have done something right since he had gone on to become a member of the Navy's flight demonstration team, the Blue Angels. (I had four students who were Blue Angels.) He was the Marine representative (besides the Fat Albert crew) and opposing solo (number 6) on the team that year. He asked if I'd be interested in a ride-along during a team practice session back home in Pensacola and, of course, I jumped at the chance. He asked the boss, Greg Wooldridge, if it would be okay and I was afforded the privilege granted to a very few. Solo VIP rides are not uncommon but spending 45 minutes in a rehearsal *is* uncommon. I thoroughly enjoyed the flight with John "Gucci" Foley, the lead solo (number 5). The most valuable thing I learned from that flight was the importance of timing for the Blues, too.

Also, the rare opportunity to sit in during the brief and de-brief afforded insight into the Blue's world that is unprecedented.

It was clear during our own briefs and de-briefs that we had successfully incorporated a similar approach into our civilian operation. I was exceptionally proud of that.

After Jim completed his aerobatic competency check with one of our evaluators (most of us were ACEs), he and I flew our first airshow together at Marine Corps Air Station Cherry Point, North Carolina, and our second at Aguadilla, Puerto Rico. Jim continued to reflect professionalism and I was pleased with his continuing progress. He clearly remembered a lot from his Navy days and our military approach to flight discipline was effective.

*Paul Entrekin & John "Gucci" Foley*

About the only time I observed Jim display poor headwork was just prior to our departure for Puerto Rico.

We each had a battery operated, hand-held, early generation GPS that neither of us was particularly comfortable with so the apprehension for this potentially internecine trip was palpable.

As we were preparing to depart Opa Locka, Florida, for our first stop in Great Inagua (the southernmost island in the Bahamas) I noticed as Jim was preparing to strap in that he was not wearing a flotation device. I had a military issue LPA and told Jim we weren't leaving until he had something adequate in case he had to ditch. This was the first (and last) foray for either of us into the Bermuda Triangle and I wasn't taking any unnecessary chances. He bought a cheap, bright yellow airline stow-under-the-seat type from the FBO and slipped it over his head. We both laughed, wondering if it would even inflate and, if it did, speculated as to whether or not he'd just be making it easier for the sharks to see him.

Aside, both GPSs batteries failed on the leg from Great Inagua to Aguadilla (out of sight of any land) and without reliable VOR navigation stations, so as the flight lead I was forced to dead reckon to our destination.

Jim flew most of his work-up flights on T. J.'s wing and I was the lead when T. J. and I flew. So, my actual flight time with Jim had been limited. Except for some minor problems on our cross country flights, from my perspective Jim's flying was fine.

What I didn't know until months later was that some folks had expressed concern over Jim recovering too low from some of his solo aerobatic maneuvers after we split from the two-ship formation aerobatics portion of the act. I was busy flying my own solo part of the routine and blissfully unaware of the bad tendencies that were developing.

Later that year, we were booked to fly the Marine Corps Air Station El Toro airshow. Except possibly for NAS Miramar near San Diego, it was the biggest airshow in southern California with live television coverage and crowds close to a half million people. With usually perfect weather, it was a primo airshow and a privilege to be considered good enough to be booked there. I had flown there previously as a solo in the MiG and was looking forward to returning.

For some reason, though, T. J. and Jim ended up being scheduled to fly the show together for the first time. Unfortunately, T. J. got really sick there and could not fly at all. The Pitts team flew a 3 ship demonstration that was a contingent for having a sick pilot or an aircraft down for unforeseeable maintenance reasons. The dogfight act had to be adjusted for the Sabre as a solo and Jim agreed to fly. T. J. said that they thoroughly briefed the adjustments that Jim would need to make to keep the jet in front of the crowd as much as possible and that, although excited, Jim seemed cool and ready.

No doubt Jim was pumped with adrenaline and ready to show what he could do all by himself . . . and he did.

After a section takeoff, we would normally make one turn in the pattern as a flight of two to clean up the gear & flaps and accelerate to appropriate aerobatic airspeed. Keep in mind that for the first part of each show Jim was *always* the wingman. In close formation he never had to rely on an interior scan to assure he had plenty of speed. He relied on his lead for that and was accustomed to almost always looking outside the cockpit until later in the show, after the split.

We'll never know why Jim decided to forego that turn in the pattern to build energy and, instead, entered his first maneuver way too slow.

Entering a loop with a roll on top, he pulled an estimated 5 to 6 Gs instead of the typical 4 to 4 ½ at a minimum airspeed of about 300 knots which would have assured him enough altitude on top to complete the maneuver. By the time he finished the roll he was doomed. Accustomed to relying on the lead to ensure the proper parameters, we can speculate that he probably never looked inside for airspeed or altitude indications that would have shown he was both too low and too slow to continue. Had he realized his predicament at any time prior to committing the nose of the Sabre below 45 degrees on the back side, he could have rolled out and recovered. He didn't, and continued to pull even though he had topped out at an estimated only 2,500 to 3,500 feet AGL—as much as 1,500 feet lower than necessary.

It was estimated that he might have made it with only another 200 feet or so, but as he saw the ground rushing toward him he pulled even harder and entered accelerated stall and impacted the runway directly on the centerline. The airplane exploded and Jim's body was thrown clear. (We were also later told that someone had noticed Jim stop, unstrap and stand up in the cockpit just prior to taking the runway. Although highly unlikely, it's possible that he didn't strap back in which, even if he didn't, would have probably had no bearing on the survivability of that crash anyway.)

The beautiful black jet named "Sabre Dance" was destroyed and Jim Gregory was killed instantly.

Because the incident occurred on a naval installation, the Naval Investigative Service (NIS—the forerunner to today's NCIS or Naval Criminal Investigative Service) became involved and, during their background check, discovered that Jim had obtained his original pilot's license by fraudulent means. He had actually attrited from advanced flight training in the TA-4 and never received his wings. Somehow, though, he managed to take the FAA's military competency exam which afforded him a commercial pilot's license.

Members of the Holiday Inn/Coca Cola Team and I were all taken to task, in particular by a couple of members of Team America (two of which are now, themselves, deceased following aircraft mishaps) who observed Jim fly previously but kept their criticisms to themselves. Had we known of his shortcomings involving low recoveries we might have been able to offer corrective guidance. Sadly, though, there was only finger pointing and blame after the fact.

As the president of ICAS, T. J. had been the driving force behind establishing new policies that made it significantly more difficult for new performers to receive the credentials necessary to fly at airshows. The ACE (Aerobatic Competency Evaluator) program had replaced the previous Performer Safety Committee and took the responsibility for certifying performers from the FAA (which, with their lack of expertise, they were glad to be rid of) in a previously unprecedented way. The result, intentional or not, basically pulled up the rope behind those of us already qualified and grandfathered in. There is no doubt it was implemented purely to protect the financial interests of those performers and their sponsors with big bucks invested in the airshow industry. The potential for the cast of available players for the playing field was shortened considerably which meant more money available for fewer folks.

I concede that I was caught up in the concept of the plans for the soon to be reality of a civilian jet aerobatic team and soundly distracted from some of the important details surrounding individuals' qualifications.

T. J. had succeeded in negotiations with Coca Cola for them to sponsor four L-39s. The conceptual drawings of the paint scheme had been approved (glossy black with Coca Cola in red) and co-sponsorship from Rolex, Ray Ban and other corporations who would supply the pilots with untold goodies for ourselves and state of the art equipment to thoroughly modernize the 80s vintage jets was already under way.

However, the plan was never brought to fruition.

Four months after Jim's crash, T. J. was killed in Kazakhstan while on a buying trip for the L-39s.

Witnesses to the incident indicated that T. J. agreed to take a Russian officer on an aerobatic demonstration flight at the base where the jets were being procured. They saw the L-39 (probably being flown by T. J.) line up for an inverted, low level pass down the runway. Whether someone's shoulder harness or lap belt came unlocked (or failed) or whether the passenger became frightened or just inadvertently grabbed the stick, no one will ever know. The result, though, whatever the cause, was the jet going straight into the ground and T. J.'s remains were shipped home in a very small FedEx container.

And so, for me at least, the dream of being a part of the first civilian jet formation aerobatic team had vanished with T. J. Brown.

The star I hitched my wagon to had burned out in a blaze of glory.

*MiG-15 flown by Paul Entrekin and F-86 flown by Jim Gregory at St. Louis*

# Chapter 10
# SWAN SONG

Up to this time, besides me, only four people had ever flown my MiG. Aside from Norman Suits who flew it twice and T. J. Brown who flew it only a few times, I also checked out former squadron mate and one of the best pilots I've ever known, Tom Archer (during our mutual relationship with Northern Lights Aircraft in Montgomery, Alabama) and my good friend (and former Canadian Air Force Snowbird) Holmes Patton. Both flew the jet sparingly.

Dirty Harry said "A man's got to know his limitations." There's a profundity in that when you think about it. I'd like to think that pilots who live to be *old* pilots have an innate sense of how far to push the envelope, whether that of their aircraft or their own.

I've always referred to that innate sense as "my little voice" and, so far, listening to it seems to have served me well.

It had occurred to me that flying a 50-something year old airplane would inevitably involve mechanical failure—hopefully not a catastrophic failure but, even with high quality maintenance, machines break.

Beyond the mechanical limitations of the jet, I had to recognize my own physical limitations as well. Even though I consider myself to be in excellent physical condition, I've known so many individuals who have died doing airshows whose mishaps were not attributable to mechanical malfunctions and the only conclusion was physiological factors, it was practical to consider how long I should continue pulling Gs.

Last year (2011) at the Reno Air Races, it is speculated that Jimmy Leeward had an elevator trim tab malfunction that caused him to be subjected to substantial G forces. It appears that he subsequently lost consciousness which allowed his highly modified P-51 air racer to crash into the crowd killing several spectators. Even though it is a logical argument to presume that most individuals would black out at the rapid onset of 10 plus Gs, he was pushing the envelope at 75+ years old.

A man's got to know his limitations.

Air racing and airshows are a young man's game. There comes a time when *bold* airshow pilots must consider their mortality and hang up their spurs so as to become *old* airshow pilots. So it was that, approaching 50 something, I began to listen to my little voice and made a plan to have an appropriate swan song performance.

Having the National Naval Aviation Museum in my home town made the choice of where to retire the MiG very simple.

Following some negotiations with the museum's director, Bob Rasmussen, we arrived at a mutually agreeable deal that would allow me to retain ownership of the jet but place it on long term loan to the museum. They had a Japanese zero and, eventually, a Me 262 but no MiGs. The inclusion of my jet would be a jewel in their crown of "enemy" aircraft.

I was invited to fly in the NAS Pensacola airshow in November and concluded that it made sense to fly my final performance here in my home town and facilitate the MiG just being towed from the ramp over to the adjacent museum.

The wheels were set in motion and the plans were made accordingly.

On my final trip home with the jet, I landed at Sherman Field and taxied clear of the duty runway. Ground control instructed me to taxi to the performer's ramp.

Upon entering the ramp area I attempted to make a minor turn and felt no response when I squeezed the brake paddle on the stick. I was moving at a relatively slow speed but realized that I had lost all brake effectiveness. To make matters worse I was heading straight for Blue Angel number 5 with no way to steer or stop.

My brakes had failed due to worn brake pucks that had either allowed the brakes to overheat and rupture the rubber bladders or puncture them with the metal keepers. The chance of both brakes failing simultaneously was beyond remote.

Fortunately the ramp was slightly up hill and the MiG coasted to a stop well before endangering the blue F-18 that filled my windscreen. I carried an expedient chock in the cockpit and used it quickly. Crisis averted.

Unfortunately I missed the practice show on Friday while waiting for the necessary replacement parts but was up and running by mid-day on Saturday. The Blues, aware of both my maintenance situation and the fact that I was flying my last show, had graciously allowed me to be last on the program. The weather was marginal but good enough for a flat show and I had a hollow feeling in the pit of my stomach as a taxied in for the final time.

The jet remained on the ramp there for nearly a month due to some last minute issues that Captain Rasmussen indicated had been raised by the museum's legal counsel. Their lawyer had concluded that the museum could not accept the "liability" for an aircraft they did not own. I was highly suspect of this reasoning due to the fact that I knew it was common for museums to have aircraft "on loan" from other museums and individuals. To further complicate the negotiations, I was told that it would be necessary for me to pay an exorbitant insurance premium with the museum as the named insured for liability. They said they were concerned that the MiG could possibly cause a fire but the question that could not be answered was how an aircraft with no battery, no fuel and minimal lubricants could possibly be the source of a fire.

I deduced that I was being strong-armed to donate the jet outright to the museum which, at that point, I found to be exceptionally bad form on the part of Rasmussen.

Although I initially had no intention of selling the jet, I had been pursued by an acquaintance of T. J. Brown's, Tobe Gooden (one of the pilots he had considered bringing on board to affiliate with the Holiday Inn team when T. J. moved to the Coca Cola jet team), who really wanted my MiG because of its historic significance.

He was a retired Air Force fighter pilot who was flying for Continental Airlines and lived near Houston.

We agreed to a price and I reluctantly decided to sell the airplane.

Aside, the National Naval Aviation Museum eventually acquired one of the original five MiG-15s imported from China and it hangs suspended from the ceiling there which causes me to look up and smile whenever I visit.

I ferried the jet to Conroe, Texas, where I was to train the new owner and provide a check-out towards his acquisition of a MiG-15 LOA. Once I had fulfilled my end of the deal I headed home with an ominous sense of dread about what I had done.

I had experienced similar feelings when I sold my Pitts, the beautiful Spectrum Eagle, to an attorney from San Diego.

The pilot he retained to fly the plane from Pensacola to San Diego (and provide some instruction en route) was, ironically, the same guy who ferried the brand new, unpainted, aircraft from Christen Industries in Afton, Wyoming to Santa Paula, California. (That same pilot had somehow managed to disconnect and drop the canopy on asphalt which caused substantial damage from scratches. The canopy was buffed to remove the scratches but there was always some minor parallax on that particular spot.)

Further demonstrating his ineptitude, he ran the Pitts out of fuel and crashed in Louisiana on their first leg. Neither was killed but the attorney had a broken leg and the plane was substantially damaged. Of course lawsuits followed and even though I was absolved of any responsibility, the ensuing litigation provided a lesson about selling anything to an attorney.

That same ominous feeling proved to be justified when I learned that Tobe was somehow now unable to pay for the MiG as agreed. After some song and dance about financing, I finally agreed to payment terms which began a multi-year odyssey with a partner I never intended to have.

Eventually, over a period of years, he paid off the debt and then abruptly obtained a partner to share expenses. I wished them well and we disassociated ourselves.

A short time later I learned that Gooden, following a fuel stop in Little Rock, Arkansas, had experienced what he thought was an "acceleration problem" once airborne during takeoff. He felt the best course of action was to put the MiG back on the runway. Unable to stop on the runway remaining, he went off the end and made an excursion through the overrun and into a nearby wooded area. The photographs I saw weeks later indicated the aircraft experienced relatively minimal exterior damage.

Like Curt Farley, he operated on a shoe string budget and had only minimal hull insurance on the aircraft.

Although I was aware of the mishap there was no reason to believe that the jet would not be repaired and flying again. What I did not know was that the insurance company paid off the claim and then sold the MiG piecemeal for parts. By the time I learned the fate of the MiG it was too late to do anything although I would have gladly bought the jet intact for salvage and then either repaired it to flying status or donated it to another museum in cosmetically suitable condition. I understand the cockpit section of the fuselage now sits forlornly in the small Air Combat Museum in Springfield, Illinois.

The end of one of the most noteworthy jets in U.S. aviation history was abrupt and unfitting of such an aircraft.

Having flown helicopters (Bell Hueys, Cobras & Jet Rangers and the enormous Sikorsky CH-53 Sea Stallion and sleek S-76), fighters (the F-5,

F-18, F-104, MiG-15, MiG-17 and MiG-21), experimentals (the BD-5J microjet, Christen Eagle and Pitts Special) and airliners (Boeing 727, 757, 767 and 777) logging time in around 50 different types of aircraft, I've experienced many realms of flight.

From flight test to flight instruction, low level airshow aerobatics at 50 feet & 500 knots, 50,000 feet & Mach 1+, and on 14 hour legs from Atlanta to Tokyo, more than 30,000 hours of my life have been spent airborne—launching from terra firma and from the pitching decks of ships at sea, recovering often times at night or with zero visibility.

After an aviation career that included signing autographs, television appearances and show promotions, government and motion picture contracts, jumping out of airplanes and shooting guns and rockets from them, spotting a battleship's naval gunfire, transporting movie stars and dignitaries and even hanging by a carabiner under a helicopter—I've had a blast.

Like most of its contemporaries, the MiG-15 now flies only in my dreams and during those ethereal occasions I allow myself to recall how surreal it was to fly. It never scared me and I was always careful to afford the respect it was due.

In a way that only man and machine can when involved in a delicate aerobatic dance or reaching into the heavens in rarified air, bonded as one and confident in each other, we soared and rolled blissfully together. Me, knowing that I was afforded a privilege seldom known by fliers and the MiG, I felt, surely sensing that it had been given a unique chance to explore a new world of flight and lauded and hailed worldwide rather than being relegated to the obsolescent anonymity of a Chinese military flight line as an extinct relic of war.

In those dreams I sit comfortably in the cockpit, never cold and shivering or soaked in a miserable redolent sweat, but soothed by the sunlight reflecting in through a crystal clear canopy that affords an awe inspiring view of a cobalt blue sky seldom seen by most men.

And I am ever so grateful to have been so blessed.

# Acknowledgments

Steve Wallace, dear friend and former Canadian Snowbirds pilot number 9, who encouraged me to pursue the fantasy of procuring and flying the first civilian-owned MiG in the world.

Bruce Goessling, who (although he euchred me out of a substantial sum of money on a subsequent aircraft deal) had the foresight to actually go to China to purchase and retrieve the first group of MiGs intended for civilian flight in the free world.

Ken Rowe (aka No Kum-Sok), the first North Korean pilot to fly "A MiG-15 to Freedom", who was of great help in sorting through some of the myths surrounding his story as well as many that evolved about the Korean War era.

Brian McCoy, Bandit number 53, whose experience with the United States Air Force's 4477th Test and Evaluation Squadron "Red Eagles" helped to ensure an accurate recounting of CONSTANT PEG.

Viktor Belenko, who risked his life to escape communism in a MiG-25 Foxbat and whose input was critical to correcting misconceptions surrounding his own life's story.

Jim Robinson, whose funding and passion and Chuck Parnall, whose tireless efforts helped to ensure that civilian owners of surplus military turbine powered aircraft could operate without undue bureaucratic interference.

Dr. Edward Noland, for his editing skills and assistance with the manuscript.

Dr. Victor Goeller, my dear father-in-law; a multi-type rated pilot and former United States Air Force flight surgeon who also edited the manuscript and shares a love of flying, history and the pursuit of truth.

My fellow airshow pilots, who allowed a warbird to share center stage.

# Professional *Curriculum Vitae*

## **CIVILIAN**

President & Chief Pilot, Entrekin Aviation
Captain, Delta Air Lines, retired
ALPA Airport Liaison Representative, Pensacola Regional Airport (PNS)
Federal Flight Deck Officer, TSA/DHS
ICAS Performer Safety Committee
CJAA Co-Founder/Vice President
Project Pilot, Northern Lights Aircraft
Pilot, Combat Jets Flying Museum
Air Boss, Pensacola Beach Airshow
Research Volunteer, National Naval Aviation Museum

**RATINGS:**
Airline Transport Pilot (Commercial)
Airplane Multi-engine Land
Airplane Single-engine Land
Rotorcraft-Helicopter
Instrument-Helicopter/Airplane
Boeing 757, 767, 777
Flight Engineer-Boeing 727
MiG-15, MiG-17, BD-5J
Level 1—(Unlimited/Ground Level) Aerobatic Competency
FAA/ICAS ACE (Aerobatic Competency Evaluator)
FAA Endorsing Authority, MiG-15/17 series

## ACHIEVEMENTS:

*United States and World Record Holder* (National Aeronautic Association & Federation Aéronautique Internationale) Speed Over A Recognized Course, Atlanta to Pensacola—505.51 mph, MiG-15bis, 7/6/93
*United States and World Record Holder* (National Aeronautic Association & Federation Aéronautique Internationale) Speed Over A Commercial Air Route, Atlanta to Greensboro—486.60 mph, Boeing 727-200, 4/6/03
*World's First Civilian MiG Pilot/Owner*
Author, *Mighty Hands—Victory Over Adversity Through the Grace of God*

## AIRCRAFT EXPERIENCE:

| | | | |
|---|---|---|---|
| North American T-6 (SNJ) | Mooney 201 | Christen Eagle II | Cessna 172 |
| Stearman | Aerospatiale A-Star | Pitts S-2A/B | Cessna 182 |
| Beechcraft T-34A/B | King Air Super 500 | Boeing 727 | Cessna 185 |
| Beechcraft Bonanza | Piper Tri-Pacer | Boeing 757 | Cessna 207 |
| Beechcraft Baron | Piper Seminole | Boeing 767 | Cessna 310 |
| Hawker Siddley 125 | DeHavilland Beaver | Boeing 777 | BD-5J |

## ORGANIZATIONS:
Society of Experimental Test Pilots
Ancient Order of Quiet Birdmen
National Aeronautic Association
National Air & Space Society
National Naval Aviation Museum Foundation
Air Line Pilots Association
International Council of Air Shows
Experimental Aircraft Association
American Helicopter Society
Classic Jet Aircraft Association

# **MILITARY**

United States Marine Corps—Commissioned, 1977
                            Designated Naval Aviator, 1980, number 15,444
Top Secret Clearance
Deployed—Marine Aircraft Group 36
              1st Marine Aircraft Wing
              Futenma, Okinawa, Japan
Detached—D.I.A. (Defense Intelligence Agency), 1986-1991
Retired—Major, USMC, 1991
Synopsis:
Operated aircraft within North America (United States, Canada), Japan, Korea, Philippines and aboard ships at sea. Flew tactical and administrative missions and transported Cabinet level officials, Flag officers and foreign dignitaries. Aviation Safety Officer (graduate—U.S. Naval Postgraduate School)

## QUALIFICATIONS:
Special Instrument rating

<u>Helicopter</u>
Squadron Pilot—Marine Light Helicopter Squadron 267 (HML-267)
                  Stingers
                  Marine Attack Helicopter Squadron 369 (HMA-369)
                  Gunfighters
                  Marine Aircraft Group 39, 3rd Marine Aircraft Wing
Weapons & Tactics Instructor Certifications—Terrain Flight Instructor
                                    Night Vision Goggles Instructor
Carrier Qualified (day/night)
Formation Leader—Section/Division/Flight
Formation Instructor
Instrument Instructor
Navigation Instructor (day/night)
Cross Country Instructor

<u>Fixed Wing</u>
Naval Air Training Command Instructor Pilot—VT-3 Red Knights
Aerobatics Instructor
Primary (familiarization) Flight Instructor (day/night)

Formation Leader—Section/Division/Flight
Formation Instructor
Instrument Instructor
Navigation Instructor (day/night)
Cross Country (high altitude) Instructor

Other
Forward Air Controller—1st Battalion, 5th Marine Regiment

**ACHIEVEMENTS:**
United States Marine Corps Aviation Safety Award
Bell Helicopter Outstanding Military Achievement Award
Order of the Red Max (VT-3)
Honorary Plank Owner, USS Iwo Jima (LPD 7)
Canadian Air Force Supersonic rating
Honorary Member—Bandit Flight (Canadian Air Force, Moose Jaw, Sask.)
Multiple Individual & Unit Awards

**AIRCRAFT EXPERIENCE:**
MiG-15bis/UTI Casa Saeta HA-200 Bell TH-57A Jet Ranger
MiG-17bis O-2A Scout Bell UH-1N/E/L Huey
MiG-21U
Bell AH-1J/T Cobra
Lockheed T-33
Lockheed F-104 Starfighter Sikorsky CH-53D Sea Stallion
CF-18B Hornet
CF-5D Freedom Fighter Beechcraft T-34C Turbo Mentor

**ORGANIZATIONS:**
Order of Daedalians
Marine Corps Aviation Association
Association of Naval Aviation
Legion of Valor

For more information about the author see:
PaulEntrekin.com
NavalAviationMuseum.org site map (National Flight Log)
Wikipedia.com (Paul T. Entrekin)

# MiG *Firsts*

First MiG flight—4 April, 1940
> I-200 prototype designated MiG-1 in December, 1940

First MiG jet flight—24 April, 1946
> I-300 prototype later designated MiG-9

First MiG swept wing jet flight—30 December, 1947, **V.N. Yuganov**—pilot
> I-310 (S-01) prototype
> S-03 prototype designated MiG-15 in 1948

First pilot to shoot down a MiG—8 November, 1950, **Lt. Russell Brown**, USAF flying a P-80, North Korea

First MiG pilot to defect—5 March, 1953, **Lt. Franciszek Jarecki**, Polish Air Force, flew to the Danish Island of Bornholm

First North Korean MiG pilot to immigrate—21 September, 1953, **Lt. No Kum-Sok** flew to Kimpo Air Base, South Korea

# AMERICAN MiG *FIRSTS*

First American to fly a MiG—29 September, 1953, **Capt. Tom Collins**, USAF at Kadena Air Base, Okinawa

First MiG in America—1953, Lt. No Kum-Sok's MiG-15, Wright-Patterson AFB Dayton, Ohio

First MiG-21 in America—1968, acquired from Israel after Iraqi Air Force pilot Capt. Munir Redfa defected in 1966, code named HAVE DOUGHNUT

First MiG-17 in America—1969, acquired from Israel after Syrian Air Force pilots 1$^{st}$ Lt. Walid Adham and 1$^{st}$ Lt. Radfan Rifai defected in 1968, code named HAVE DRILL (first) & HAVE FERRY

First MiG test squadron in America—1969, 6512$^{th}$ "Red Hats", Edwards AFB, California

First MiG aggressor squadron in America*—1977, 4477$^{th}$ "Red Eagles", Groom Lake, Tonopah, Nevada
(*The Foreign Technology Division or FTD, based at Wright-Patterson AFB, of the Air Force Systems Command or AFSC and the 414$^{th}$ Fighter Weapons Squadron exploited the MiG-17 and MiG-21 in 1973 as a precursor to CONSTANT PEG.)

First MiG-23 in America—1977, acquired from Egypt, code named HAVE PAD

First American MiG importer—1985, **Doug Champlin**, Champlin Fighter Museum, Mesa, Arizona
3 MiG-15s from China

First American to own/fly a MiG—1987, **Paul Entrekin**, Entrekin Aviation at Mojave, California
1 of 5 MiG-15s from China

First MiG airshow performance in America—1987, **Paul Entrekin**, Paine Field Everett, Washington (*Also flew first MiG airshow performance in North America, 1987 Abbotsford, British Columbia)

First American to own/fly a MiG-17—1988, **Dean Martin**, Warplanes, Inc. Burlington, Vermont

First American to own/fly a MiG-21—1990, **Jim Robinson**, Combat Jet Museum Houston, Texas

First person to set a U. S. Airspeed record and
First American to set a World Airspeed record in a MiG—1993, **Paul Entrekin**
Atlanta to Pensacola

First American to own/fly a MiG-29—2010, **Don Kirlin**, Air USA Quincy, Illinois

# Author's References

Rowe, Kenneth H. (aka No, Kum-Sok) with J. Roger Osterholm. *A MiG-15 to Freedom*. McFarland & Company, Inc., 1996.

Wolfe, Tom. *The Right Stuff*. Farrar, Straus & Giroux, 1979.

Yeager, Chuck and Leo Janos. *Yeager*. Bantam Books, 1985.

Davies, Steve. *Red Eagles, America's Secret MiGs*. Osprey Publishing, 2008.

Zuyev, Alex with Malcolm McConnell. *FULCRUM, A Top Gun Pilot's Escape from the Soviet Empire*. Warner Books, 1992.

Barron, John. *MiG PILOT, The Final Escape of Lieutenant Belenko*. McGraw Hill, 1980.

Belyakov, R. A. and J. Marmain. *MiG, Fifty Years of Secret Aircraft Design*. Naval Institute Press, 1994.

Oliver, David. *MiG Dynasty*. Motorbooks International, 1990.

Gordon, Yefim and Vladimir Rigmant. *MiG-15, Design, Development, and Korean War Combat History*. Motorbooks International, 1993.

Zaloga, Stephen J. *The Russians in MiG Alley*. Air Force Magazine, 1991.

Wetterhan, Ralph. *To Snatch a Sabre*. Air & Space Magazine, 2003.

Bergin, Bob. *Mission: Bring Down The Spy Plane*. Air & Space Magazine, 2012.

Maloney, Edward T. *Russian MiG-15*. Planes of Fame Publications, 1995.

Butowski, Piotr with Jay Miller. *OKB MiG, A History of the Design Bureau and Its Aircraft*. Midland Counties Publications, 1991.

Gunston, Bill. *Chronicle of Aviation*. Chronicle Communications, Ltd., 1992.

Taylor, Michael J. H. *Jane's Encyclopedia of Aviation*. Portland House, 1989.
O'Leary, Michael. *Jet Warbirds*. Motorbooks International, 1990.

Gunston, Bill. *Aircraft of the Soviet Union*. Osprey Publishing Ltd., 1983.

Mason, R. A., Air Vice-Marshal and John W. R. Taylor. *Aircraft, Strategy and Operations of the Soviet Air Force*. Jane's Publishing Company Ltd., 1986.

Green, William and Gordon Swanborough. *The World's Great Fighter Aircraft, The inside story of 100 Classics in the evolution of fighter aircraft*. Crescent Books, 1981.

Gunston, Bill. *The Illustrated History of Fighters*. Exeter Books, 1983.

Sweetman, Bill. *The Presidio Concise Guide to Soviet Military Aircraft*. Aerospace Publishing, Ltd., 1981.

Spick, Mike. *Jet Fighter Performance, Korea to Vietnam*. Motorbooks International, 1986.

Hallion, Richard P. *The Naval Air War in Korea*. The Nautical & Aviation Publishing Company of America, 1986.

Rabinowitz, Harold. *Conquer The Sky, Great Moments In Aviation*. Michael Friedman Publishing Group, 1996.

Park, Edwards. *Fighters, The World's Great Aces and Their Planes.* Thomasson-Grant, Inc., 1990.

Gunston, Bill. *Aviation: the first 100 Years.* Barron's Educational Series, Inc., 2002.

Austin, Alan and Anthony Dicks. *Great Fighting Planes, World War I to the Present Day.* Octopus Books, 1985.

Boyne, Walter J. *The Smithsonian Book of Flight.* Orion Books, 1987.

Taylor, Michael J.H. *Jet Warplanes.* Bison Books Corp., 1984.

Rabinowitz, Harold. *Pushing the Envelope, Airplanes of the Jet Age.* Michael Friedman Publishing Group, 1998.

Sweetman, Bill. *100 Years of Flight.* Publications International Ltd., 2002.

Walker, Bryce. *Fighting Jets* (Epic of Flight series). Time-Life Books Inc., 1983.

www.ingramcontent.com/pod-product-compliance
Lightning Source LLC
Chambersburg PA
CBHW030525080526
44586CB00011B/330